"*Ravelings* beautifully knits together the complexities of the head, the entanglements of the heart, and the all-too-human hungers that hit us right in the gut. These essays delve into the rich contradictions of singleness and connection, balance and chance, fullness and lack—always with a sense of wonder and intellectual grace. Thoughtful, poignant, and beautifully written, this is a book I will return to again and again."

—RANDON BILLINGS NOBLE, author of *Be with Me Always: Essays*

"You want to go deep into Lisa Knopp's essays. They're not meant for a quick read. Detail is all. Like the impressionists she refers to, each one is itself, often without need for a story. Yet the rich story of her life runs through like a stream—the death of a beloved cat, the death of parents, eating doves, the comfort of a giant sweet potato, consulting the almanac, finding a lost car. These beautifully written essays are a record of a life lived with sensitivity and wisdom. Her essay 'Still Life with Peaches' is a map for how to see, how to find words for close-seeing. I couldn't put this book down."

—FLEDA BROWN, author of *The End of the Clockwork Universe*

"Lisa Knopp's essays invite us to notice the things of daily life while pointing us to what shimmers just beyond our line of vision. Knopp is clear-eyed and reverent as she harnesses examples from art and etymology, memory studies and theology, to explore loss, aging, and the rich layers of human appetite. These essays embody the holy work of paying attention, of forging connection and of letting go. A luminous, tender collection by a master of the form."

—SONJA LIVINGSTON, author of *The Virgin of Prince Street*

"In this collection of virtuoso essays, Lisa Knopp puzzles and ravels topics ranging from encountering her mother's dead body to dancing with a broom. The lowly sweet potato, the exalted peach, the art of Renoir and Lassnig, all warrant her probing consideration. The essay on a familiar feeling with the little-known name of velleity is one of many startling discoveries lifted from the ordinary. With every deep dive into these streams of her life, we vibrate like a tuning fork, resonating and enriching our understanding of the intricate balances and delicious contradictions of everyday life."

—PAMELA CARTER JOERN, author of *At the Corner of Past and Future: A Collection of Life Stories*

Praise for Lisa Knopp's *The Nature of Home: A Lexicon and Essays*

"An abiding devotion to a place and its inhabitants: sentimental in the right way, mnemonic, tempting."

—*Kirkus Reviews*

"We must include Knopp among those whom Barry Lopez calls our 'local geniuses of the American landscape.' . . . Knopp understands that what is essential is always with us. Knopp understands the nature of home."

—FRAN SHAW, *Parabola*

"*The Nature of Home* displays Knopp's native gifts as an essayist, including her ability to take the most quotidian of moments. . . . and glean from them important insights about the ways we live."

—JONATHAN RITZ, *Great Plains Quarterly*

"Knopp demonstrates the value of making a commitment to one's place and becoming acquainted with its inhabitants, from the bulrushes in the salt marsh to the neighbors next door. *The Nature of Home* conveys the importance of striving to understand and preserve our home places."

—ANGELA WALDIE, *ISLE: Interdisciplinary Studies in Literature and Environment*

"A significant treatment of home, environment, and natural history. It succeeds on several levels: as an observant work of regional nature writing, as a thoughtful collection of interlinked essays, and as a moving book of personal reflections. . . . It has the breadth and vision of Thoreau's *Walden* and the intimacy and integrity of Scott Russell Sanders's *Hunting for Hope* while still maintaining its own unique identity and its author's individual voice."

—ROBERT ROOT, author of *E. B. White: The Emergence of an Essayist*

Praise for Lisa Knopp's *Interior Places*

"[A] smart sequel to Knopp's earlier study, *The Nature of Home*. . . . Rapt observer, botanist, birder and chronicler of the human condition, Knopp is also, in the best literary tradition, a wanderer of lingering curiosity. . . . Elegiac, soulful and discerning."

—*Kirkus Reviews*

"*Interior Places* is a great sample of local nature writing, making it ideal for academic study or for those who want to start reading creative nonfiction."

—RYAN BORCHERS, *Omaha World-Herald*

"In these engagingly written pieces Knopp describes the people and places of Nebraska, Iowa, Ohio, and, in one essay on the famous flier Amelia Earhart, Atchison, Kansas. Her recounting of a visit to the aviatrix's birthplace, interspersed with town history and an account of Earhart's equal dedication to flying and serving the urban poor (the latter manifest in her work with the settlement house movement of the early twentieth century), demonstrates Knopp's method of looking closely at geographical spaces as windows upon more interior places." —*Kansas History*

"Although Knopp focuses on the Midwest, her writing should interest readers who desire to live a life informed by the flora, fauna, geology, and history of the region where they reside."

—LISA WOOLLEY, *Bloomsbury Review*

"Whether watching wood ducks with naturalist Aldo Leopold's brother Frederick or contemplating the quotidian lives of two of P. T. Barnum's circus giants, Knopp's observations have been finely honed over time and place into purposeful explorations of themes that have percolated throughout her childhood and finally come to fruition in her adult roles as writer and professor, mother and daughter."

—CAROL HAGGAS, *Booklist*

"It is always a pleasure to read Lisa Knopp's prose. Not only does it flow smoothly, but it offers wonderful visual images. This is a book that makes me pause while reading as I mentally make a list of the people to whom I will be giving it as a gift."

—BECKY FABER, *Great Plains Quarterly*

"These new essays are mostly set in Iowa and Nebraska; in each, the author moves easily from the concrete to the abstract and back again, blending history, science, personal reminiscence, observation and reflection—inspired by topics such as the formation of geodes, memories of her grandmother, bird-banding at Schramm State Park, volunteer work among the poor, or her experiences with claustrophobia. . . . Knopp demonstrates again why she is one of Nebraska's most respected essayists."

—*Nebraska Life*

"Lisa Knopp's quietly significant *Interior Places* is surely among the more important essay collections of our millennium's first decade."

—GAYNELL GAVIN, *Western American Literature*

"Lisa Knopp explores the inner life—subjectivity—with grace, compassion, and a love for landscapes. This book brings together two of the major currents in creative nonfiction—memoir and nature writing—from the mature perspective of a writer dedicated to careful inhabitation. Like those geodes that open this fine collection, *Interior Places* sparkles all the way through."

—ELIZABETH DODD, author of *Prospect: Journeys and Landscapes*

"Knopp is one of our finest American natural history writers. There's no writer I know who is better at capturing the beauty and detail of the tallgrass prairie and plains states. Knopp writes lyrically yet scientifically with her facts grounded in both experience and solid sources. She now takes her place among such writers as her literary mentor Aldo Leopold."

—MARY SWANDER, author of *The Desert Pilgrim: En Route to Mysticism and Miracles*

Ravelings

AMERICAN LIVES

Series editor: Tobias Wolff

Ravelings

Essays on Love, Loss, and Wonder

LISA KNOPP

University of Nebraska Press

Lincoln

Acknowledgments for the use of copyrighted
material appear on page 189, which constitutes
an extension of the copyright page.

The University of Nebraska Press is part of a land-grant institution with campuses and programs on the past, present, and future homelands of the Pawnee, Ponca, Otoe-Missouria, Omaha, Dakota, Lakota, Kaw, Cheyenne, and Arapaho Peoples, as well as those of the relocated Ho-Chunk, Sac and Fox, and Iowa Peoples.

For customers in the EU with safety/
GPSR concerns, contact:
gpsr@mare-nostrum.co.uk
Mare Nostrum Group BV
Mauritskade 21D
1091 GC Amsterdam
The Netherlands

Library of Congress Control Number: 2025022268

Designed and set in Minion Pro by L. Welch.

CONTENTS

PREFACE

A contronym—a word with a pair of contradictory meanings—is a curiosity. The verb "ravel," for instance, means "to disentangle" threads or strands. But an older, less common meaning is "to entangle" them. One must consider the entire sentence in which the word appears to determine if "raveling" means "to make" or "unmake," "to complicate" or "simplify." Other contronyms include "cleave" ("to sever" or "to adhere to"); "outstanding" ("excellent" or "remains to be done"); "bound" ("restrained from movement" or "moving toward a destination"); "apology" ("a statement of contrition for" or "the defense of an act or belief"); "weather" ("to withstand" or "to wear away"); "fast" ("moving quickly" or "firmly attached"); "sanction" ("to permit" or "to condemn"); "left" ("remained" or "departed"); and "puzzle" (if you "puzzle over" a problem, you're trying to understand something that perplexes or confuses you; if you "puzzle out" a problem, you're trying to resolve it through careful thought or investigation).

The intended meaning of such Janus-faced words may be apparent, as in the following sentence: "My mother would ask one of us to hold the skein while she raveled it into a ball, which was easier for her to pull yarn from when she was knitting, and less likely to ravel than yarn pulled from a skein." But in other cases, even the most careful attention to the sentence in which the word is embedded doesn't reveal which of the contradictory meanings the speaker or writer intends, as in this line from the Scottish poet Edwin Morgan: "Nothing more dazzling than a raveling plot."

The women in my mother's family were ravelers. From my mother's paternal grandmother, I inherited a Depression-era double wedding ring quilt and from her maternal grandmother, a Sunbonnet Sue from the same era. I also have a quilt from Greataunt Pertise, who went her own way, machine stitching polyester squares cut from her old pantsuits into simple, heavy quilts.

My mother and grandmother worked with yarn, a more fundamental craft than quilting, since knitting and crocheting have the same end: creating fabric by pulling loops through loops. My mother, who lived boldly and defiantly, was a consummate knitter. When I was thirteen, I gathered a basket of her artistry—cardigans and pullover sweaters with single and double cable stitches or complex geometric designs; mittens; and argyle socks, all in classic colors—and entered them in the Des Moines County Fair. She kept the stack of blue and red ribbons; I kept the small cash prizes she won. In contrast, her mother, an unadventurous homebody, was freewheeling with the pattern instructions and didn't seem to care what colors she used, as if she was color blind or as if consistency and taste didn't matter. What resulted are creations that remind me of the rebelliousness of African American improvisational "crazy" quilts—asymmetrical swatches, brash and surprising color juxtapositions, dissimilar borders. I treasure the several afghans of hers that I saved.

Though my mother taught me to knit and Granny tried to teach me to crochet, I lacked the desire or discipline to master either. But turning lines of text into a woven whole has long drawn me. While some of my essays are a straightforward single line, most tangle and untangle, complicate and clarify. They puzzle as they ravel. And so, the same ravel of text can explore both the blending in a single moment of the exotic and mundane, of fullness and want, of love and abhorrence, of desire and contentment, of freedom and bondage, of severance and connection, and of the creative act as both an evocation and an imposition. The essays in this collection consider these antitheses and, in some cases, reconcile them.

I wrote these essays over a sixteen-year period, with the oldest being "Kaddish," about the rituals I enacted in response to my father's death in 2006, and the most recent being "Faith, Bone Deep," written in late 2024 and early 2025 about my efforts to reverse my osteoporosis. Some essays are discursive in that they digress or ramble; others are discursive in that they proceed logically and coherently toward a conclusion. But most contain a bit of both approaches. All are freestanding, written with no thought of how they might work together in a collection. But they *do* work together in capturing how one can be transformed by great and small encounters with love, loss, and wonder, by puzzling over and puzzling out the meanings of such encounters, by noticing or discovering the points of connection.

When selecting the essays for this collection, I had more than twice as many as I needed. I gave preference to those that are more focused on my experiences as an older adult than as a child or young adult, and that contained in varying proportions the same three themes of love, loss, and wonder. I tried sequencing the essays in various ways according to subject, theme, and mood, but in the end, what felt right was rather chronological, ordering the essays according to when the dominant experience in that essay occurred. And yet, when essays insisted on being paired together because of similar themes, concerns, or imagery, I honored their request and broke with chronology. For the most part, I've retained time references appropriate to when I wrote each essay rather than bringing them (my age or that of my children, for instance, or the number of years since an event occurred) up to date.

Although this is a work of nonfiction, I've slightly altered the names and circumstances of some of those I've written about to protect their privacy.

Ravelings

In the Place of Their Exile

A couple of times a week, I walk in the neighborhood just south of East Campus, the agricultural campus of the University of Nebraska–Lincoln. Before I began working on this essay, I would have told you that I walk that old neighborhood because I find more architectural and botanical diversity there than I do on the newer streets near my house. But now I know that it's more than the tree canopies, curbside gardens, dignified old homes, and run-down student rentals that compel me to walk this neighborhood a ten-minute drive from my house.

I begin my walk near a red brick fourplex, built in the late 1940s or early 1950s. I know the layout of 3525 Apple Street, the apartment on the lower west side: a living room; a small kitchen, once a mild yellow, I think; a hallway; a bedroom behind the kitchen. The floors are hardwood. I don't remember the bathroom. The former rail bed of the Missouri Pacific Railroad, now the "MoPac," a bike and pedestrian trail, drew the southern boundary of the backyard.

My family lived at 3525 Apple Street for at least six months that I can verify, though seven or eight is more likely. I turned five while we were living there. In the winter of 1960–61, my father was laid off from his job as a laborer at the Chicago, Burlington, and Quincy (CB&Q) Railroad shops in West Burlington, Iowa. He took a similar job at the shops in Lincoln. I want to modify the verb "took," but any adverb I pick—gratefully? grudgingly? expectantly? reluctantly? hopelessly?—would be speculation, though my parents may have felt each of these sentiments in some measure.

They found tenants for the Cape Cod house in Burlington they'd recently bought, packed up, and moved 350 miles west. Briefly, they rented a room with a kitchenette in an old house shadowed by the Nebraska State Capital Building. My only memory of that dark place that reeked of something revolting, like cooked cabbage, is of my mother arguing with the gaunt landlady about the saucers of rodent poison on the floor of the room where my younger brother and I played. Next, we moved into a furnished basement where the kitchen was so tiny that we ate at a table in the living room. Jamie's crib was in my parents' bedroom, but I can't remember where I slept. We lived close enough to the shops that when Jamie and I heard the quitting time whistle, we ran to the corner to pick out from the stream of men pouring out of the yard—each in steel-toed boots and dirty overalls and toting a dinner bucket—our father's loose hipped, out-toed walk, his brown hair parted on the side and combed over like Cary Grant's, and his hazel eyes which found us before we found him.

That basement apartment was a dispiriting place. It was dark and a place of sickness, since Jamie and I both had hard measles and I had scarlet fever there. Thereafter, my mother had an aversion to basements—like the cheap, mildewy one where my son and I lived in Macomb, Illinois while I earned my master's degree; my son's bedroom when he was a teenager in Lincoln; the hospice room in Ohio where she died. "I don't want to be in a basement," she mumbled between doses of morphine. I turned her bed so she could see that the sliding glass door opened onto a patio; beyond that was a pond and woods. When I told her about the trees, she smiled, though I doubt that I had convinced her that the lowest floor wasn't really a basement.

Compared to the other two rentals, the Apple Street apartment was a clean, bright, decent place, a relief, even though my parents may have slept on a fold-out couch in the living room so Jamie and I could have the bedroom and, supposedly, an old man had been injured or killed on the train tracks in our backyard. Shortly after we moved in, we went to a stately home on Sheridan Boulevard, even now a grand place where Lincoln's old money lives, to buy a bed for me. While there, my mother fell in love with an antique Windsor chair and persuaded the owners to sell it as well. It may have been the first of the many antiques she would acquire. I had a sore throat and was sucking on a Luden's cherry cough drop, a taste that I still associate with that time when I entered the most magnificent house I'd ever seen.

As I reflect on how unsettled and discontented my parents were during their sojourn in Lincoln, I feel such love, compassion, and sadness for them. My mother was twenty-five and twenty-six, which now seems so young to me. For her, the disruption and anguish of moving beckoned memories from her childhood. Because her father was an ironworker who followed the jobs in the southern Great Plains, he, my grandmother, and mother moved frequently, often as soon as the school year ended. Mom and Granny spent seemingly eternal summers in cities where they knew no one until school started and so filled their idle, isolated days by devouring stacks of comic books. Because my grandparents never owned property or stayed at one address very long, my mother craved a permanent home with ballast—several acres of land, trees she'd planted and named, jammed-full closets and cupboards, hard to move antiques, walls crowded with framed photographs of her children and grandchildren, and plenty of pets (at one point, five dogs, two horses, a cat, geese, ducks, sheep, and at an earlier point, rescued box turtles with cracked shells and wild birds with broken wings).

My young mother wanted so much. She was captivated by John Glenn's launch into space which she watched while seated on the Windsor chair directly in front of the TV. She sent the poem that she wrote about "the housewife that soared with Captain Glenn," while leaving behind "a house in disarray" to a newspaper (*Lincoln Journal Star*? Burlington *Hawk Eye*?) that chose not to publish it. Years later, she worked the metaphor of Glenn's moon launch into her often-told story about why she returned to college and became a teacher, a story that included a recitation of her poem. But when we lived on Apple Street, the meaning of Glenn's orbit may have been more overt: she wanted to be launched into space where she could escape the gravitational pull of housework, childcare, isolation, boredom, and homesickness.

During my parents' Lincoln Era, my father turned twenty-nine. After serving with the U.S. Army in Korea, Dad hoped that he'd never have to leave home again. He had simple needs: the grounding and familiarity of the place where he'd grown up and where both sides of his remarkably untraveled family lived (it was a rare Knopp or Freiberg who left Des Moines County for anything other than military service), where he proudly worked at the railroad which bore the name of our hometown, where he had workbenches in the basement and garage, and he fished in the Mississippi and the Skunk Rivers. While other people lived in our Cape Cod, a town where we were within a ten-minute drive of most of his relatives, in Lincoln we made do in a sparsely furnished apartment in a riverless city where we weren't related to anyone. My father, too, was forlorn during this time and place of weathering, both that which erodes or wears away and that which brings one safely through.

I searched through boxes of photographs for images from my family's Lincoln Era. Since my mother always photographed my brothers and me with our birthday cakes or Christmas presents or on the first day of school or at extended family gatherings, I was perplexed when I only found six. But perhaps she hadn't wanted to memorialize our time in such deficient and temporary quarters. Two of these photos show Jamie and me doing acrobatics in the yard outside of a house with white, asbestos-cement siding, a dark gutter pipe with peeling paint, not-yet blooming tiger lilies, and the door that led to our burrow. (How my mother must have dreaded descending those steps!) Since the photos are dated May 1961, this must have been the house near the railroad shops. Two other photos were taken in front of the Apple Street fourplex when my uncle and aunt from Burlington visited. Jamie and I stand beside them, dressed in our Sunday best; behind us, the tailfins on our aquamarine car. In another photo, Dougie, the stout little rough neck who lived in the apartment across the hall from ours, posed with us. In my kindergarten school picture, my blonde, pixie-cut hair has straight clean parts and a white barrette on the left. I wear a red and green plaid dress trimmed in white. My smile is wan or wary. I remember my mother walking me to school under a railroad viaduct that is no longer there on a day when dry leaves skittered in the wind. I remember Miss Pardee reading a book to my class in which umbrellas were called "bumbershoots," a word I loved to say. While writing this essay, I discovered that Bernice O. Pardee retired in 1971 after twenty-two years at Hartley Elementary. I am consoled and shaken when I find that memories of mine that seem like they're too far back in time to be accurate actually are.

As I feel my way back into this time, I retrieve memories of life at 3525 Apple Street that surprise me with their vividness, specificity, and metaphoric potential. One that I treasure is of me studying by the glow of my night-light, the patterns on the double wedding ring quilt that Great-grandma Parris had stitched covering my bed. I bestowed on the print fabric squares descriptive names, perhaps my earliest search for germs of stories in what I was given, perhaps my earliest attempt at name-staking. Now when I look at those worn, faded patches, I imagine the names that I might have brought forth for them when I was five: raining daisies and bumbershoots; blue kitty tic-tac-toe; rings around the rosie; candy stripe parade.

After fourteen long, homesick months in Lincoln, my father took a welding job at the J. I. Case Company in Burlington, where he worked until he was rehired at the West Burlington shops, this time as a boilermaker's apprentice. Since there were still several months remaining on our tenants' lease for our Cape Cod house,

Dad lived with his mother in Burlington, while Mom, Jamie, and I lived with Mom's parents forty-five miles away in Keokuk, Iowa, during what was my grandparents' most settled period. I finished kindergarten at Wells-Carey Elementary with Miss Bertha Paul, who had taught my mother twenty-one years earlier. I hated going to school, got daily stomachaches, cried for Mom and Granny, and begged to go home. "If she says she's sick, we'll just treat her like she is," Mom told Granny, and sent me to my little bed in the room that I shared with my grandfather who read blueprints and erected steel frameworks by day and snored loudly at night. Being stuck in bed while Mom, Granny, and Jamie were having fun downstairs was still better than being at school without them.

I don't know what my parents' marriage was like during the Lincoln Era, but I know what it was like later. My mother was the center of attention, the one in the crowd that you couldn't stop watching. Her blue eyes were large and expressive; her hair was red and curly; her body thick and solid, despite her yo-yo dieting. She was smart, witty, and loquacious, laughed and cried easily, and danced often and with abandon. My mother said that she "wanted it all," though that was impossible given her colliding desires. She didn't want to be a housewife, a boilermaker's wife, and neglected many aspects of domesticity and conventional marriage. But she loved her home and her children, and she loved to knit and cook. I have clear memories of her culinary creations, both foods that I loved (iced butterhorn rolls; sweet, limp bread and butter pickles; creamed chipped beef on homemade biscuits; firm, nutty fudge; crispy corn fritters dipped in syrup; fried potato cakes, soft inside and crusty on the outside; and her specialty: fruit and cream pies, the latter tall with meringue), as well as those that I didn't like (goulash, pot roast, ham and beans, beef stew, chili). But I don't remember anything that she cooked during our Lincoln Era. When she was thirty, the year in which her third child was born and she kept the medical records at a hospital, my mother entered college so that instead of chasing defiant dust bunnies, she could soar with Captain Glenn. Being a biology teacher suited her: the classroom was her stage; her audience adored her, which made our family rather famous in Burlington. In contrast, my father was quietly, dutifully there. He spent the rest of his working days as a boilermaker at the West Burlington shops. After work, he bought groceries, vacuumed, swept, did laundry, cut grass, paid bills, tended the animals, followed shifts in the weather, and tried to ignore his wife's infidelities. My father aimed for little and got little in return.

About a year before she died, my mother and I were chatting about how those aspects of my personality that I'd most like to change—a tendency to be moody, too critical of myself and others, and skeptical of my own power—work against me. She mentioned something, not really to me but as if she were musing out loud, that puzzled me. She said that when we moved to Lincoln, I was a happy, carefree, confident child. But when we returned to Burlington in time for me to enter first grade, I had become the type of person that I am now. Did something happen to me in Lincoln, I asked? Or was it in Keokuk? Or was the personality I was born with becoming more set and apparent? My mother didn't know, didn't even have a theory. I've speculated causes, but it feels careless, dangerous even, like I might be creating or beckoning something that I won't want to live with but that once unloosed would be impossible to contain. Since I'd rather live with a gap than with something that might be false or harmful, I've backed off.

I don't feel this degree of melancholy about other times and places from my childhood or that something essential is missing from the stories I tell or silently carry about them. Nor do my memories of other times arouse such compassion in me for my parents, ordinary flawed people each with their own wants and needs, who did their best given the dislocations, the financial pressures, and their mismatched personalities. I hoped that by writing about my family's Lincoln Era, I would uncover the cause for the shift in me that my mother alluded to. Yet, my probe of this period and the few months that we lived in Keokuk hasn't revealed even a shadow of an inciting event. Might I have become this person even if my father had never gotten laid off by the most desirable employer in our hometown and had to leave his home and widowed mother for a place that could never compare? Might I have become this person even if my mother never had to exchange her first real home, the one with chandeliers in the living and dining rooms, her secretarial job, the women she met with to play bridge and discuss the fat novels they read, and her family nearby for rented rooms where she was cooped up, bored, and broke? Or was the inciting incident simply this: my parents were unhappy, and because I loved and depended on them, that touched me deeply?

There is no one living who can answer my questions. Yet the emotions I feel as I write and that cling to me even when I'm not directly working on this essay offer clues. Psychologists say that when we store memories, we store both the event (receiving the hoped-for gift or embarking on the long-awaited trip) and our mood at the time of the event (delight). But the *type* of mood we experience affects which memories we can access. We more easily and reliably recall a memory when the mood within that memory matches our mood at the time of recall than when there's a mismatch between the two. So, it's easier to remember details about the events surrounding an expected and desired invitation that never arrived and our subsequent devastation when we are sad than happy. Mood-congruent recall, it's called. Likewise, we more easily and reliably bring forth memories when our mood at the time of retrieval matches our mood at the time when the memory was stored, regardless of the content. I remember coming home from middle school to find my mother waiting for me on the front porch wearing her new glasses. While the content of this memory is neutral and seems insignificant, it arrives packed in pleasure and contentment, though I don't know why. (Was I delighted to find her at home waiting for me when usually I came home to an empty house? Had I had a really good day at school?) And so, I'm more likely to retrieve it when I'm happy than sad. Mood- or mood-state-dependent recall, it's called.

When I reenter that long ago time, memories arise that I didn't know I had. Perhaps so few of them are happy because of what I feel now: sorrow over the deaths of my parents; regret over the divisions between my brothers and me over matters related to the settling of my mother's estate; regret over the 23andMe revelation of the identity of one brother's biological father, a secret that I'd carried for too long. Also contributing to my melancholy are my ruminations about whether, after I retire, I should remain in this adopted hometown, where I have good friends but just wisps of family history, or return to my first hometown, where I have few present-day connections but thick layers of family history and plenty of ghosts, some of which are quite pleasant to encounter, others less so. How I envy those who have both of aspects of home in one place and don't have to choose which they'll do without.

But there is another reason why I remember what I do. Psychologist Martin A. Conway says that one of the important functions of what he calls the "working" or "conceptual" self is making more accessible memories of experiences that are in harmony with one's current goals, self-image, and beliefs, while making less accessible memories of experiences that threaten, contradict, or undermine the coherence of one's "self-system" or that would require substantial changes in it if those memories were to be accommodated. This process is one of the reasons why we remember some moments in our past with clarity and detail while others are hazy or accompanied by the disquieting sense that we've forgotten something essential. I suppose this is why, when I imagine myself at four and five, I see a younger version of the angsty, self-doubting person that I am now rather than the easygoing, self-assured child that my mother described.

I don't mind gaps, surmises, or uncertainties in the autobiographical stories others tell *if* the teller acknowledges them. In *Where the Past Begins: A Writer's Memoir*, Amy Tan explains that at age sixty-five, and without conscious choice on her part, her "brain has let a lot of moments slide over the cliff." While writing her memoir, Tan was aware that much of what she thinks she remembers "is inaccurate, guessed at, or biased by experiences that came later." If she was to write the same book years later, she'd describe some events differently, "either because of a change of perspective or worsening memory—or even because new evidence has come to light." The latter occurred when Tan's mother told her about the guilt that her late father felt for having loved a married woman. This revelation called into question Tan's long-held perceptions of her family.

Tan, author of *The Joy Luck Club* and other novels, sees striking similarities between fiction writing and an aging memory, in that both are "impressionistic and selective in details." Her "fictional mind" required that while writing her memoir, she let go of "logic, assumptions, rationale, and conscious memory." Rather than "sticking to what really happened," she embraced "whatever [came] to mind" and was guided by her intuition as she created her story. And yet, while examining photos, letters, and other artifacts, Tan was gratified to learn that many of her childhood memories were largely accurate and, in many cases, returned to her in full. I appreciate her honesty about how she filled the gaps in her story and her methods of reconciling her memories and the facts with her conceptual self.

But when the teller doesn't acknowledge her omissions, I feel excluded or deceived. In *The Gastronomical Me*, M. F. K. Fisher withholds information about the suicides of her brother, David, and of Dillwyn Parrish, her second husband and love of her life. As much as I love Fisher's fresh and insightful reflections, sumptuous prose, and zesty spirit, I am frustrated by these gaps. In *Poet of the Appetites: The Lives and Loves of M. F. K. Fisher*, Joan Reardon explains the conspicuous omissions of details about Dillwyn's and David's deaths in *The Gastronomical Me* by quoting from Fisher's journal about this devastating time: "There are too many things that I cannot write yet. They're in words in my head, but I am afraid of writing them. It is as if they might make a little crack in me and let out some of all the howling, hideous, frightful grief. It is difficult to know, certainly, how to live at all." How much more trustworthy Fisher's memoir-in-essays would be had she acknowledged that she wasn't yet ready to open her wounds and tell the whole story. But instead, she withholds.

I won't fictionalize to fill the holes in the story I tell about the first time I lived in Lincoln. Nor will I ignore them—if I'm aware of them. But I will speculate about what my feelings reveal as I walk past 3525 Apple Street. I am sad about my parents' circumstances and even sadder about their having left Lincoln. Because they were deeply unhappy, longed to flee, and finally did from the place that has been my home for well over thirty years, I feel betrayed and abandoned—an illogical, childish response, since they couldn't have known that one day I'd settle in the place of their exile. But feelings aren't rational. Theirs is a different type of truth.

My mother, who craved hilly, wooded landscapes beneath smaller skies, never understood my commitment to this flatter, drier prairie place. "Why on earth would you want to live in Nebraska?" This from a woman who built her retirement home in rural Ohio. In truth, there are many places that I find more desirable than a riverless city in the Great Plains. But surely, my family's early interlude here influenced my decision to settle in this place far from my hometown and birth family. Perhaps I returned to Lincoln because I hadn't yet integrated that slim chapter about the time when my parents and brother also lived here into the story I was constructing of my life. Or perhaps I found a welcome measure of continuity in knowing that I have at least a trace of family history in this place, even if it isn't a comforting or grounding one.

The practical reason why I settled here is that the only doctoral program that I applied for in 1988 and that offered me a teaching assistantship and tuition remission was the University of Nebraska–Lincoln. Once in Lincoln, marriage and children attached me more deeply and firmly to this place than I realized. After I divorced, I took a good job in Illinois, where I, too, experienced the anguish of living in a place that wasn't home. Three homesick years later, I returned to the place that had been foreign, hostile soil to my parents. Now, I have weighty reasons for staying: diverse friendships; a dynamic church; a son who lives nearby; a faraway daughter who "comes home" to this place; a house that I love; a job that is too good to leave, especially at my age. Or perhaps I chose this place over all others based on what rarely results in a sound decision: an act of rebellion. I am here because my parents found it to be an alien and antagonistic place. I have proven them wrong.

When I walk the MoPac Trail, I can't see the back of 3525 Apple Street, because of a new rental complex near the trail. But when I walk on the street, I see our former residence clearly. For a long time, I only glanced at it and let the memories it beckoned pass quickly. But now when I look, I muse upon what the girl who lived there long ago has to do with the woman walking past. Sometimes, I glimpse my beautiful, spirited mother stepping out the kitchen door to hang wet clothes on the lines or to shake the dust mop with a vengeance. Or I see my handsome, stolid father sitting on the front step smoking a cigarette as Jamie and I pedal past on our tricycles. I watch us on payday tote bags of groceries from Hinky Dinky into the place that wasn't home, while my mother playfully sang what I now know is a risqué World War I drinking song, "Hinky Dinky Parley Voo." These images move me beyond words. I want to embrace and assure each of us that all will be well, and for the most part, it will be. But sometimes, I see us carrying boxes, suitcases, my bed, the crib, couch, quilt, TV, and Windsor chair from 3525 Apple, fitting them into the rental truck and our aquamarine car, and locking the apartment door for the last time. My father returns to double check the lock as he would with any door that he locked for the rest of his life. I want to call out and ask us to stay. But I know not to interrupt. At that moment we are happy and hopeful. Finally, we're going where we'd rather be.

Kaddish

On the day my father died, I dug sweet potatoes for the first time. The chartreuse foliage that had overrun a quarter of my garden had blackened and withered with the first hard frost. Had I heeded the frost dates listed in the *Old Farmer's Almanac*, I would have dug the tubers before October 10. By waiting until October 24, I risked my sweet potatoes going bad, or so Dad told me. As I dug, my fork tines snapped the red-violet roots, each a bright surprise in the black earth. But I didn't uncover a single potato. My impulse was to call Dad and ask him how far down I should dig to find what I was looking for. But my father was gone, and the late October sun was setting. I set the pitchfork in the garage and promised myself that I'd try again the next day. But I didn't. The weather turned cold, and I had a graveside committal and family gathering to attend 320 miles away in southeastern Iowa.

When I returned to work seven days after my father's death, I made the 120-mile round-trip commute between my home in Lincoln and the University of Nebraska–Omaha where I worked, with a store-bought sweet potato, big enough to feed six, reclining in the passenger seat. Surely this mammoth potato, probably the result of a long, warm, southern growing season, was many times the size of my still-buried potatoes. Even so, I found the coppery skin and the swollen, crescent-shape of my grocery store potato homey and comforting. Occasionally, I picked it up by the middle, where it was so thick that four full inches separated my thumb and middle finger, and hefted it. When I stopped at red lights, I studied the corky, gray-brown scars; the dark, raised flecks; the dozens of craters, some scarred and sprouting whiskers, some clean indentations in the thin, leathery skin; and the dry, ashen "navels" at either end. One navel was puckered and sunken; the other, where the swollen tuber had been cut from the nutrient-carrying umbilical cord, was a gnarled tip, bent down like the top of a stocking cap. A shallow gash about two inches long revealed the orange flesh within. Soon, that too would form a gray-brown scar.

~~~~~

Ten years earlier, my recently retired parents moved from our hometown of Burlington, Iowa to rural Ohio to be near my brothers, both of whom had found jobs and settled in the Cleveland area. Shortly after they arrived there, Dad was diagnosed with intermediate-stage prostate cancer. The doctor predicted that the disease would kill my father in two to three years. Six years later, the cancer had metastasized in his spine and collarbone. Shortly thereafter, he was accepted into a clinical study at Cleveland Clinic where he received one experimental treatment after another, some of which may have slowed the growth of the cancer and one of which almost killed him. But Dad believed in his doctors and the treatments they prescribed and because of his faith, lived almost a decade beyond the first doctor's prediction.

I expected my father to continue to defy the odds. But on September 11, 2006, following the seventh of ten doses of radiation, his doctor said that there would be no more treatments and recommended hospice care. This news hit me harder than that of his death six weeks later. When I was at home, I was almost always aware that my father was being wrenched from us. I cried often. On the days that I had to go to Omaha to teach or sit through meetings, I'd push down thoughts of my father's imminent death. But when I got in my car for my commute home, the grief bubbled up in me. Once I entered the fast anonymity of the interstate, I'd wail and sob. "Dad, Dad. This can't be happening to you—to us."

After purging my sadness for the time being, I'd pray for healing. Of course, my father had to die someday, and this appeared to be his time. But at least it could be a good death—whatever that meant—and God could give those of us who loved my father strength and comfort.

On weekdays, Hospice of Wayne County, Ohio helped with Dad's care. But on the weekends, my parents were alone. My brothers, Jamie and John, and I agreed that one of us should be there on weekends and any other time that we could spare. When I arrived for my first shift on September 28, I was surprised to find my father thin and frail, and with dark bags beneath his eyes. His voice was weak and elderly, and he was easily confused. Each morning, my mother and I lifted him out of bed, careful of his catheter and urine bag and his painful lower back, and into a wheelchair. Once in the living room, we'd ease him into his recliner. There, he'd doze and rouse, watch the Channel 5 News, "The Martha Stewart Show," or the horse auctions on RFD-TV, pick at a plate of food, stuffing what he didn't want to eat between the cushion and the side of the chair, and drop off again, sometimes in mid-conversation. In the afternoon, we'd lift him into his wheelchair and take him back to bed. My mother gave him pills to make him sleep, pills to lessen his anxiety, and pills to ease the pain. Could this really be happening to him—to us?

In the evenings, Dad laid in his hospital bed and read or watched ball games. I sat on a chair beside him, reading student essays, stopping often to chat.

"How's your garden?" he asked during one of these pauses.

"Better than last year's. You remember what that looked like. The rain came at the wrong time, so I had all that foliage but hardly any tomatoes or peppers. Good beans, though. This year's garden is better, except the rabbits ate the beans."

"You get plenty of tomatoes?"

"Plenty. But never enough."

"Gourds?" Dad called acorn squash "gourds."

"The dogs ate the gourd leaves so I'm down to one plant. I tried sweet potatoes, too." Each year, I planted something that I'd never grown before. The previous year it was eggplant. The year before, Dad, my daughter, and I planted rhubarb. The year before, okra.

"Did you dig 'em yet?"

I shook my head.

"They'll go bad if you don't get 'em out of the ground before the first frost." He gave a firm nod for emphasis.

"Don't worry, Dad. I'll dig 'em when I get home."

He returned to his ball game, and I returned to my students' essays until the next commercial.

"Remember those sweet potatoes I grew on Lower Augusta Road? Man, those were good. I kept them in boxes in the basement. We had enough to last all winter." I did remember. Sometime in the early 1980s, a holiday dish became a staple at my parents' house. They baked sweet potatoes the way they'd once baked Russets. "One year I went out to dig sweet potatoes and the moles had ate 'em all." Dad shook his head. That year, my parents bought sweet potatoes, not the normal, fist-sized ones from the backyard garden, but behemoths from the grocery store, like the one that rode in the passenger seat of my car for almost a month following Dad's death.

I returned for my second shift on October 13, the day after my father's seventy-fourth birthday. How does one celebrate the birthday of a dying man? I brought a box of Russell Stover chocolates, in hopes of fattening him up, a Barbara Mandrell ball cap that I'd found at our church yard sale (Dad liked her songs "Sleeping Single in a Double Bed" and "I Was Country When Country Wasn't Cool"), and the 2007 *Old Farmer's Almanac*. The latter was a traditional gift. Almost every year for either his birthday or Christmas, I'd buy him the almanac for the upcoming year. By the end of the year, the almanac was fat, dog-eared, and spattered.

The almanac has deep roots in our family. When I was a child, my dad's mother kept one on a hook by her kitchen sink. Before she planted vegetables or cut her hair, she'd consult the almanac to determine if the placement of the moon in the zodiac was propitious for such an activity. On at least a couple of occasions, she showed my brothers and me "The Man of Signs," the frightening drawing of a naked man with a grim face and a quartered abdomen. Lines connected the symbols of the zodiac signs that encircled the flayed man with the corresponding body parts. My grandmother said that according to "The Man of Signs," those born under Aries's influence had trouble with their heads. In her case, that meant dizzy spells. In Jamie's case, that meant earaches and allergies. As Virgos, John and I could expect to have trouble with our bellies, and indeed we do, though a couple of decades would pass before that predisposition was made manifest in me. As a Libra, Dad was to have trouble with his "reins." The line connecting the scales, the symbol of Libra, to the splayed man pointed to the place where his thighs met his abdomen. I didn't know what kind of problems one might develop there.

Shortly after my twentieth birthday, my grandmother died. Perhaps that is when Dad started buying his own copy of Robert B. Thomas's almanac, "published every year since 1792," as it proclaimed on its busy gold cover. Though Dad wouldn't be planting potatoes in 2007, and though he probably didn't need to read the forecasts about the severity or mildness of the upcoming winters for the Lower Lakes where he lived or the Heartland where I live, I knew that he would want to read the articles ("The New Old-fashioned Way to Farm"), glance at the recipes ("Death Row Bourbon Sauce" for barbecue or baked beans), study the advertisements (the electric-hydraulic Dr. Wood Splitter which "Splits logs up to 16″ . . . indoors or out"), and the home remedies ("Troubled by cracked lips? Massage them with a dab of earwax—preferably your own"). I hoped that the almanac, with its predictable cycles and homespun, earthbound wisdom would comfort us at this time of final harvest and approaching winter.

When I bought the almanac, it was an effort on my part to close the gap between my father and me. We had never been close. In fact, I don't know if he had been close with anyone. Too many people who should have loved and supported him had hurt him, and so he kept his distance, even from his own children. During the final years of his life, I was determined to get to know him. But it wasn't easy. My father spoke little, revealed little, and rarely asked the kind of questions that showed interest in another—in me. And now, I wonder what questions he might have wanted me to ask of him. For most of my adult life, when I telephoned my parents, I'd talk to my mother. But once Dad's cancer metastasized and time seemed so short, instead of asking her about his medical condition, how he felt, what he was doing, I'd ask her to pass the phone to him. He'd answer my questions with brief answers—"Good."; "Okay."; "Ah, you're nuts." The questions he asked me were predictable and skin-deep—"Is your car running good?" "How's the garden?" But I would try to get him talking about how he was spending his day, what was happening in our old hometown (I even got him a subscription to our hometown newspaper), or something from his childhood or mine. "Well, we better get off the phone, Lisa. This is costing you money," he'd interrupt a few minutes into our conversation, as if cell phone calls were charged by the minute. My brothers reported the same phenomenon. But at least he and I were briefly talking on the phone several times a week.

When I bought the 2007 issue of the *Old Farmer's Almanac*, I imagined that Dad and I would read the articles and look over the calendar pages together. Not the left-hand pages with their complicated charts about when the sun and moon rose and set, the declination of the sun, the sun fast (the best time for resetting your sundial!), the place of the moon in the sky, and the high tide times in Boston, a city which neither of us had visited. Rather, we'd study the right-hand calendar pages with their curious old symbols for the various planets and celestial events and ornate capital "S's" to indicate which days were Sundays. I imagined us commenting on the anniversaries: "October 21: Timber rat-tlesnakes move to winter dens." ("Seems late, don't it?" he'd say. "Think they're talking about those rattlers that live near Boston?" I'd ask.); "October 26: Minimum wage raised to 75c per hour, 1949." ("What did they pay you when you worked at the gas station in high school, Dad?") We'd nod over the wisdom of the aphorisms, such as "Never look for a worm in the apple of your eye." ("Everybody's a little wormy," Dad would say.) Even before we knew about these red-letter dates, October was a significant month in our family, with Dad's birthday on the 12th, that of my son's estranged father on the 13th, and that of my sister-in-law on the 15th. The last week of October was also important. Because the public schools in Lincoln closed for teacher-in-service days, my children and I often visited my parents that week, returning to Lincoln in time for Trick-or-Treat Night. But if we ever needed another October holiday, the almanac offered plenty of choices. The right-hand page listed the feast days of Frances of Assisi, Luke, Simon, Jude, and others, as well as the movable feasts of Yom Kippur, Sukkoth, and Ramadan.

I hoped that as Dad and I read the almanac together, we'd reminisce. We'd start with our various gardens from the one that his parents tended ("Ma made everything from that garden—sauerkraut, root beer, catsup.") to the huge garden on Lower Augusta Road near Burlington, where he tended brussels sprouts, gourds, strawberries, white and sweet potatoes, and more. My mother toiled in a steamy kitchen, putting up so many jars of tomatoes, corn relish, pickles, and jelly that the laundry room shelves bowed with their weight. When I lived in Des Moines, Dad not only planted his own garden, but bought me a pitchfork and shovel and helped my son and me plant our first one. When my parents moved from the Lower Augusta Road house, Dad never again planted a big garden. But he was always curious about mine.

We never read the right-hand pages together. The first and only thing I read to Dad from the almanac was "Best Fishing Days and

Times." Apparently, the article contained nothing that he didn't already know. "Give me that book," he said, grabbing the almanac before I had a chance to start reading the "Tackle-box Checklist." He flipped through the pages until he settled on an article. The blue Barbara Mandrell cap sat tall on his head.

"Do you remember that ocarina that you had when you were a kid? Grandma called it your sweet potato pipe." I could see the hollow, elliptical plastic ball with open finger holes and a small mouth tube. "Grandma kept it in that dresser on the back porch with all of her Cracker Jacks prizes. Did you ever figure out how to play that thing?"

I looked over to see the almanac folded on his chest and his eyes shut.

When I left my father on October 17, I was hopeful. If Mom and I helped him out of bed and provided a steadying hand, he could follow his walker into the living room. Rather than using the commode in his bedroom, he followed his walker into the bathroom and used the toilet. The doctor and hospice nurse had helped my mother find a combination of drugs that allowed Dad, and thus anyone else in the house, to sleep through the night. On Sunday, October 16, a brilliant, sunny day when the trees in northeastern Ohio were at their peak color, I drove my parents to a harvest festival in nearby Sterling, Dad's first outing in over a month. He sat in the backseat with the window down, sipping coffee, listening to the band, and watching people while Mom and I bought apples and "gourds." With the surge of strength and lucidity that we saw in him, my mother was confident that she could take care of him alone the following weekend. John would take the weekend after that and John's wife the one after that. I wasn't scheduled again until mid-November. Perhaps Dad would be walking unaided when I returned.

But on October 22, he started dumping blood into the toilet. Apparently, the blood thinner that he'd been taking since his open-heart surgery fourteen years earlier was not working as it should in his malnourished, radiation-weakened body and had caused what the doctor supposed was an intestinal bleed. The next evening Jamie called. "This is a hard call to make," he said gravely. "We either have to take Dad to the hospital for blood transfusions or let him bleed to death at home. What do you want to do?" The hospice nurse said that the latter would take a few hours, perhaps a few days, and it wouldn't be painful. Bleeding to death seemed more merciful to all of us than the misery of the growing cancer in his spine and collarbone, which the doctor guessed would end Dad's life sometime between Thanksgiving and mid-December. And so the death-watch began, with Jamie and my mother at Dad's bedside, and, since there weren't flights that could get us to Cleveland before noon the next day, John at his new home in Texas and me at mine in Nebraska. When I spoke to my father at 10:00 p.m., he was pleasant but confused, his speech slurred from his sleeping pills. Apparently, he knew nothing of the decision that we'd made about how his life was to end. I slept fitfully. Around three or four o'clock, I finally sank into a deep, dream-filled sleep.

When I awakened on the morning of the 24th, there were two messages on my answering machine, and a message and six missed calls on my cell phone. My father had died. I called my mother to learn the details of their last night together. She and Jamie had been with him until a little after three in the morning when they went to bed. When Mom checked on Dad at 6:30, she found him dead, though still warm. We cried, expressed our relief that his suffering had ended, and began planning all that had to be done in the next few days.

After I got off the telephone, I made tea and oatmeal for breakfast. As I was cleaning up afterward, I was suddenly overwhelmed by the conviction that my father was present in my kitchen. "Stop what you're doing and talk to him," God said. I obeyed. I repeated my claims of love, our last words to each other the night before.

I told Dad how glad I was that he had looked in on me before he left and how relieved I was that his ashes would be buried in our hometown in Aspen Grove Cemetery, near his parents, grandparents, aunts, uncles, brothers, cousins, and grandchild. Someday, my remains would be there, too, not far from his. But in the meantime, I'd tend to his grave. Then he was gone, as was the yellow light that had filled my kitchen while he was there. I sensed that Dad was proud that he had found his way to my house for this brief, final visit. In hindsight, I wish that I had talked less or simply listened. But he may not have had anything to say, even at a time like that.

I resolved not to fritter away the day that my father took his last breath and entered my home for the last time. I would go to the Catholic cathedral downtown and sit in the dark, fragrant mystery, so exotic to my Protestant sensibility, because it was most likely the only church in the city that would be open to the public on a Tuesday morning. It would be comforting to hear the old people in the front pews muttering ancient, formulaic prayers as they fingered their loops of beads. Then I'd hike the prairie at the nature center, my old haunt and home of sorts, a place I found comforting with the repeated cycles of departures and returns, growth and decay, death and rebirth. But I did neither of these. Instead, I spent much of the day talking to my mother and brothers on the telephone, emailing people at work about the classes I'd be missing, and emailing a woman at my hometown newspaper about the details of Dad's obituary. Busyness. By mid-afternoon, I was frustrated. I hadn't done anything to make the day sacred. I took a long walk in my neighborhood, came home, grabbed the pitchfork that Dad had bought me twenty years earlier, and as the sun was setting, began digging for sweet potatoes. Whether I found any or not was beside the point. What mattered was that the act linked me with my father and that it would be unforgettable.

Every time I heard a train whistle, used my shovel and pitchfork, glanced at the photo in my living room of my young, handsome father holding me when I was a baby, opened my kitchen junk drawer (so like his except that mine doesn't smell of pipe and chewing tobacco) caught an image of myself in a reflective surface (I have his loose-hipped walk, his overlapping upper teeth, his rather bulbous nose), or played the saved message on my answering machine ("Lisa, this is your dad and I thank you for the belt very much."), I would remember him. Yet I feared that eventually, I'd forget. Because of the expense of airfare to Ohio and back for my son, daughter, and me, we'd only seen Dad once or twice a year for the past decade. Since I saw him so seldomly, his passing had changed little in my work-a-day life in Nebraska. The eleven days that I spent with him in late September and mid-October and the six days the preceding July were more than I'd seen him in any one year during the past decade. I was stocked up. What would I miss now that Dad was gone?

My mother was grieving the loss of a daily presence. When she opened the closet to grab her coat, there were his. If she built a fire in the fireplace, she did so with wood that he'd cut and stacked. When she went to vote, she saw his signature in the ledger from the previous election. She confronted his absence minute by minute. But what would I miss? I seldom asked my father for advice, since his response to every problem—personal, medical, spiritual, economic, and political—was "We'll just have to wait and see." As a boilermaker, he worked on the railroad from 7:00 to 3:30, five days a week for forty-one years; as a writer and professor, I spent too much time at home to be working very hard on anything, in his mind. So, I shared little about that part of my life. What interested me the most, stories from his childhood and mine, he shared reluctantly, sparingly, and only with great prompting. What would I miss?

When I returned home from the committal service, friends

and colleagues asked how I was doing. "Most of the time, I'm okay," I answered. But I spilled the details to one colleague. The funeral was over, my father was in the ground, everyone had gone home, and I was back in my daily routine. How was I to keep his presence and absence before me? "Come into my office," she said, "and let me tell you what Jews do."

As my colleague described a lengthy, highly elaborate mourning process, I knew what I needed: a plan and a discipline that would acknowledge my father's absence and give me something to do for him. The process my colleague was describing, rooted in the experiences of Joseph, Moses, Aaron, Job, Ezekiel, and others, had been observed by many millions of bereaved for thousands of years. Why had we Protestants turned from the wise guidance that Hebrew scripture and tradition provided on this subject? I learned that for seven days following the burial, the deceased's family stayed home together and "sat shiva." During this time, the mourners neither worked nor left the house; visitors prepared meals and offered them condolences. Except for the books of Job, Lamentations, and the more doom-filled passages in Jeremiah, reading the Bible was discouraged since God's word was delightful and this delight would distract one from one's sorrow. The mourner's job was simply to grieve and remember. How grateful I would have been for a solid week of sitting shiva with my family. Two days after Dad's burial, my family scattered; four days after his burial, I was in the classroom leading a discussion of "The Inheritance of Tools," Scott Russell Sanders's essay about his father's death. Soon, the phone calls between my brothers and me that had been so frequent and sustaining during Dad's illness stopped, though my mother and I talked daily.

During *sholshim*, the thirty-day period following the burial, mourners may leave the house though they don't yet resume full activity. One wouldn't, for instance, attend a party, get married, wear new clothes, shave, or cut one's hair during this time. If it was a parent that had died, the mourner might still wear torn clothing to represent his or her grief. Sholshim is a hairy, somber, reflective time. The final period of formal mourning for those grieving the loss of a parent is *avelut*. During this eleven-month period, the mourner returns to full activity, though it's still too soon to pursue amusements. Each day, one recites the Kaddish, the mourner's prayer in the synagogue and studies a portion of the Torah. When the twelve months of mourning are complete, one moves on with life. My colleague loaned me her copy of Maurice Lamm's *The Jewish Way in Death and Mourning*, an almanac of sorts, about the signs and seasons of the year of mourning and how to use that knowledge to live well. I began reading that evening.

What wisdom there is in taking an entire year to mourn and remember. During the first year following my father's death, I moved through a sequence of poignant anniversaries: Thanksgiving ("How big a turkey did you get this year?" he'd always ask); Christmas (for a moment, I thought about buying him a pair of fine leather gloves); New Year's Day (one takes last year's almanac off the hook and replaces it with that of the new year); Easter and the arrival of spring (winter and Republican presidencies seemed interminably long to Dad); Father's Day (I'd sent him a Germans from Russia cookbook); the anniversary of my July visit, the last time I saw him before he entered hospice (despite his weakness, Dad accompanied my mother and me to museums and restaurants); my September 4th birthday (we were still hopeful about his chemotherapy); his September 11th entrance into hospice care (my hardest period of grieving); his birthday (for his next to last birthday, I gave him a sturdy, leather belt that I thought he'd wear for many years); his death and burial. Through it all, each evening before I shut out my light, I planned to pray the Kaddish: *Magnified and sanctified be His great Name. In this world which He has created in accordance with His will, may He establish his kingdom during your lifetime.*

Lamm describes this ancient Aramaic prose-poem as "a call to God from the depths of catastrophe, exalting His name and praising Him, despite the realization that He has just wrenched a human being from life." Wrenched. The perfect word for the occasion. Lamm also says that the Kaddish is a consolation *to God*, who is also lamenting the death of a loved one. Of course, the God who notes the fall of every sparrow and knows the number of hairs on the heads of each of his billions upon billions of children knew of my father's death. But the thought that God, too, was grieving this death surprised and consoled me. Lamm said that the sages believed "the whole world itself, as it were, is maintained because of [the] recital [of the Kaddish], and that it redeems the deceased, specifically from perdition." Just by uttering this powerful prayer, I was influencing my father's well-being in the afterlife. Some evenings, the prayer poured from my depths, and I exuberantly proclaimed the words; other days, it was but a handful of words that I mumbled. But no matter what, I prayed it, grateful for its ability to create in me a sense of both presence and absence, loss and fullness.

One evening just a few months after my father's death, I forgot to say the prayer. It happened when I was giving a reading at a bookstore in Iowa City and spending the night in a motel. Though I had brought the printed prayer with me, I forgot to say it, I suppose, because of the departure from routine that travel brings. When it occurred to me the next morning that I'd forgotten to pray the Kaddish, I panicked. Dad needed me and I'd let him down. But at the same time, it also felt all right not to have said it. My father's death wasn't as raw as it had been, and the words of this ancient, deeply rooted prayer had turned my gaze from the dead to the living. On *yahrzeit*, the one-year anniversary of Dad's death, I once again said the Kaddish. Then I cleaned up my garden, took down the fence and placed it in a neat coil behind the garage. My year of mourning had ended.

I found other ways to keep Dad's presence and absence before me. When I was a child, someone, my mother perhaps, cut a sweet potato in half, submerged the cut side in a saucer of water, and sat it on top of the refrigerator. Beautiful chartreuse vines cascaded down the side of the refrigerator: spring green in the dead of winter. I created the same effect in my kitchen. For Thanksgiving, my daughter took the sweet potato that had accompanied me on my commutes and errands following my father's death and made two sweet potato pies in remembrance of her grandfather. Each time I went to the grocery store, I bought sweet potatoes. Sometimes I baked them whole, letting the heat of the oven split them open so that the soft sweetness oozed out. But more often, I added chunks of them to soups, stews, and stir-fries, a culinary flourish that I learned from my former husband, who grew up in the Caribbean eating foods with African and East Indian influences. I appreciate how a salty broth balances the strong, starchy sweetness of the potato, and I like fishing the orange chunks from a soup or stew. During the winter, I studied the *Old Farmer's Almanac*, beginning with 1984, the oldest volume in my collection and the year of my son's birth, through 2007, as I planned and dreamed about my next garden. In the spring, I considered defying cemetery regulations and setting a planter on Dad's grave with a couple of sweet potato plants in it. The bright foliage would spill out of the planter and blanket the still raw earth above Dad's buried remains. By summer's end, the tuberous roots would burst the pot: my father's own crop of sweet potatoes.

In April, when my father had been in the earth for a little over five months, I began preparing my bumper crop of sweet potatoes. Like the Kaddish, this act recalled to me my father's passing and redirected my attention to the world of the living. It was a ritual that abounds in metaphors. Listen.

It's foolish to plant sweet potatoes until a couple of weeks after the last frost date, which the almanac listed as April 27 for southeastern Nebraska. Even though global warming ("global *warning*," Dad called it) has pushed that date up, I followed the dates listed

in the almanac. I prepared the ground in my garden in mid-April:
at Earl May Nursery and Garden Center, I bought Georgia Jet and
Vardaman, two popular varieties of sweet potatoes. I consulted
my almanac for the best dates for transplanting, both according
to the moon's astrological position (when the Moon is in Cancer, Scorpio, or Pisces) and its phases (the best time for planting
underground crops is during the new moon.). In 2007 that was
May 16, a slim window of opportunity, but one that I honored.
Everything else had to wait.

For several weeks, most of the growth was beneath the ground
as root systems plunged, branched, took hold. My duty was not to
despair but to have faith and keep watering. Occasionally, I lifted
or turned the vines, because where the nodes came in contact with
the soil, they produced roots, which could sap nutrients from the
main root, resulting in runty potatoes.

For the first several weeks, I was vigilant about weeding during
these early days, so the big storage roots wouldn't have to com-
pete for water and nutrients with the weeds. Then, I put my hoe
away, since the rather heart-shaped leaves were tall and vigorous
enough to shade out the weeds. I kept a sharp eye out for the
beetles, weevils, nematodes, worms, and mice that feast on sweet
potato leaves or roots, and I collected non-poisonous methods
for ridding my garden of pests, just in case I needed them. Then,
I waited for the pretty blue morning glory–like flowers. That I've
yet to see one isn't unusual, since sweet potatoes require high day
and night temperature if they're to bloom.

Dad said that I could start harvesting small potatoes from
the outermost roots in late August. The longer I left them in the
ground attached to the roots that fed them, the larger they'd grow.
But if I waited until after the first killing frost on or around October 10, I'd harvest potatoes gone bad with fungal decay, brown
pulp, or root shrivel. Several days before the first hard frost, I cut
from the roots the seven tubers, each barely a single serving, barely
enough for a meal for my children and me, from the roots and left

them in the sun to dry. Then I put the coppery spuds in a shoebox on my kitchen counter and covered them with newspapers. In this warm, humid place, the potatoes cured, and the wounds scarred over, sealing out diseases. After a couple of weeks of curing, I again wrapped each potato in newspaper to trap moisture released while still allowing the roots to breathe. Then, I sat the box in the laundry room. When Thanksgiving arrived, we ate baked sweet potatoes, as we remembered our father and grandfather, and as I gave thanks for deep roots, the assurances of a time-tested prayer, and the reliable rhythms of the Earth and the Moon.

Still Life with Peaches

On the counter dividing my kitchen from my dining room is a wide straw basket brimming with bills, receipts, greeting cards, and newspaper clippings. Hooked over the rim of the basket is a dry turkey wishbone. To the right of the basket is a white saucer that holds a flat, elephant-shaped clay incense burner, a closed white book of matches, the stub of a stick of incense, and a curl of ash. In front of the basket and saucer are six peaches, each clefted, each more oblong than round; their yellow skins are touched with red, and each one looks ripe.

Though I listed the peaches last, they're probably what you'd notice first if you saw this scene or the visual representation of it that I would make if I could paint or sketch. If I positioned a person—say, my daughter—on the other side of the counter so you could see her dark, wild hair, her bright brown eyes, and her lean form, she would command your attention and my painting would be a portrait instead of a still life.

The common, ordinary domestic objects in some still lifes look deliberately, even elaborately, posed. Those in others look as if they were chanced upon—"found" scenes the artists saw as worthy of aesthetic consideration. Because fresh ripe fruit has been a staple of this genre since the earliest expressions of the form, I immediately recognized the peaches on my kitchen counter as fitting for a still life. But, too, the peaches were the center of my attention because in so many ways I'd invested them

31

with significance. The other objects in the scene had been relatively inconsequential, attracting my attention only if I needed to dig through the basket to find a receipt, or if company was coming and I wanted my house to smell like sandalwood instead of stir-fry, or if a situation had arisen that called for wishes as well as prayers. Yet, once I recognized the peaches as the focal point of an imagined painting and began writing an essay about it, I elevated the status of everything else from the quotidian to the exceptional.

I move the peaches so that there is a clump of four in front of the basket and two to the right. I try other combinations—three and three, two and four, one and five. For my taste, the less contrived and more natural the presentation the better. But at this point, natural is no longer possible. I put the peaches in a bowl. Then I take them out in two handfuls, as I might if I'd just returned from the grocery store with a bag of fruit, and set them on the counter in two clumps about six inches apart: a contrived natural. I turn some of them over so that they are showing their pale-red or deep-red sides. Now, I'd have a range of colors to work with, if I were painting this scene. No matter how I position the peaches, everything in this grouping appears to be waiting, held in the perpetual present.

If, in still life, the selection of objects is fundamental, it's worth my while to consider what else I could have placed on the counter as an object for my imagined painting. Apples instead of peaches, for instance. An apple is a patient and forgiving fruit, willing to keep in the bottom of the refrigerator for weeks, while a peach soon wrinkles and becomes rubbery or brown and mealy. An apple picked at the heart of the harvest season speaks to me of humility and hardiness, a ripe peach of desire and fragility. I've sometimes had more fresh apples than I could eat, but never enough fresh peaches.

Next to the delicate, perishable peaches I could place a geode, an orb that will endure for many millennia. The exterior is plain, bumpy, and gray brown. But if it is cut the hollow interior shows itself to be lined with dazzling pink, purple, white, or amber. This juxtaposition might lead you to meditate on permanence and immutability, or on other interiors, both those that are revealed and those that are not. So, too, if I allowed a fly to rest on one of the peaches or included one pocked with peach scab. First, you'd see the chosen object; then you'd notice the signs of decay, a reminder of the energetic forces working beneath the skin of any living or recently living organism. This might intensify your longing to be fully present not only to the still life, but to whatever else you're experiencing in the moment—the breeze through the open window, the cat brushing against your ankle, the rattle and grind of a garbage truck, the imagined scent and taste of peaches.

If I were to cut one of the peaches in half and position it so that you could see the deeply sculpted red-brown seed husk, from which red streaks radiate into the yellow flesh, the scene would become even more striking. The kind of saucer on which I placed the cut peach would influence your perception of the scene: A shiny, black, octagonal plate? Beige stoneware graced with a golden sheaf of wheat? Tivoli china embellished with a border of delicate pink roses and blue shells and with a gold-edged rim? A red, white, and blue paper plate?

My choice could nudge my still life a little closer to cultural or anthropological record or to an expression of my social position—yet I bought all but the paper plates at yard sales, paying more for the black plates that I bought from a farm woman who purchased them new at Wal-Mart than I did for the set of china I bought from a woman in her mid-fifties who had recently lost her home, had been living with her daughter for the past several months, and then, for reasons she did not explain, was being asked to leave. I was so moved by her story that I paid her more than she was asking for the china, though not what it was worth. A still life can't convey any of this—nothing about that woman's daughter, nothing about mine.

EQUIVALENT

In front of the basket is a clump of three peaches, overlapping so that you see only the one in front, the one with the stem, in its entirety; to the left of the basket are three peaches almost in a row, with little space between them. Each is yellow-skinned and ruddy. Ravines and glowing hills. Clefts in the flesh and blushing cheeks. The weave in the basket forms zigzagging rows stacked atop each other. The sharp corner of a pink envelope juts above the curved rim of the basket. The wishbone, light, greasy, yet dry, with a chunk of gristle clinging to the tip, balances on the rim. Afternoon light filters in from the northern window to the left of the arrangement. Faint shadows. An earthy yet ethereal fragrance. Such stillness.

This last is what I most want to capture on paper.

Realism, with its emphasis on an accurate, precisely detailed, unembellished representation of the subject, is a genre of painting that rarely appeals to me. Georgia O'Keeffe, a painter of rather surreal still lifes featuring weathered bones, lurid flowers, and pearly seashells, famously said, "Nothing is less real than realism. Details are confusing. It is only by selection, by elimination, by emphasis that we get at the meaning of things." Against the wall on the same counter as the peaches are an electric can opener and a stereo that I've chosen not to include in my still life.

It wasn't just meaning that O'Keeffe was after, but feeling. In a letter she drafted in 1937 in response to what she judged to be the incorrect conclusions some critics had reached about her work, she said, "Even if I could put down accurately certain things that I saw & enjoyed it would not give the observer the kind of feeling the object gave me—I had to create an equivalent for what I felt about what I was looking at—not copy it."

I might paint the equivalent of what I felt when I viewed my still life with peaches as shimmering and impressionistic, or monochromatic and cubist, or chalky and abstract. Even so, I'd want it to be representational enough that people would recognize the objects not only as peaches, but as desirable ones at that, and my kitchen would be judged a humble, familiar place.

THE ABSENCE OF NARRATIVE

Perhaps the oldest still life with peaches is a fresco from the House of Red Deers, a villa in the Roman village of Herculaneum, destroyed by the eruption of Mount Vesuvius in 79 CE. *Peaches and a Glass Jar* is a curious painting. All the objects in it are positioned on shelves—a convention of Roman still lifes. Three green peaches are poised on the upper shelf; on the lower shelf are two green peaches and a water-filled carafe, a weird transparency within a transparency. The peaches don't seem at rest, and one is on the verge of falling off the top shelf. The carafe also seems unsettled, its curves out of whack, almost giving it the appearance of movement. A bowed twig with eight dark green leaves leans against the shelves, crossing the entire painting, bottom to top. Four of the peaches are still attached to it. Someone has taken a bite out of one detached peach, revealing the rust-colored pit, and laid the chunk on the shelf next to it, probably because the fruit was too green and unyielding to be edible.

The arrangement of the objects seems contrived, yet their weightiness is evenly distributed and the curved, diagonal sweep of the peach branch contrasts nicely with the horizontal shelves. What I find peculiar are the proportions: the peaches are almost as big as the carafe, which is composed of misshapen ovals. But in spite of these distortions, I enjoy this painting simply because the side-by-side shades of rust and lime green please me.

Some still lifes are visual sermons, thick with religious and allegorical symbolism. *Still Life: An Allegory of the Vanities of Human Life* by the Dutch painter Harmen Steenwijck features two slightly open books, traditional symbols of human knowledge; several musical instruments, symbols of sensory pleasures; a Japanese sword and a conch—rare items in early seventeenth-century Holland, and so symbols of wealth; a chronometer, an extinguished

lamp, and, near the center of the arrangement, a human skull—
all symbols of the fleetingness of human life. There is no explicit
narrative here, yet for those who can decode the iconography the
scene is saturated with meaning. In the case of *Peaches and a Glass
Jar*, the only narrative or meaning I can extract, slight though
it is, concerns the rejected bite of peach. But if we look beyond
the frame, there is that paradoxical story about the eruption of a
volcano whose molten lava both destroyed the cities of Pompeii
and Herculaneum and preserved slices of Roman life.

Typically, when viewing a still life, one has no expectation of a
story. In the relative absence of narrative, the things that matter
are shape, hue, texture, placement, and overlap of objects; the
structure of negative space; the juxtaposition of tall and short,
curved and angled, bright and dark. Whenever viewing my imagined still life with peaches, I ease myself into a state that the poet
Mark Doty calls "agenda-less alertness," above or beneath words,
names, analysis, and reflection. There I experience nothing but
the physicality of the six peaches, the basket of bills, the incense
burner and curl of ash, the wishbone, the afternoon light, and
myself as observer.

LIKE SALT OR LOVE

Still, I love the pressure to turn a cohesive setting of objects—or
a connected sequence of events—and the reflections they inspire
into a narrative, a form and movement that people easily recognize
because it's ancient and natural, and so something we crave, like
salt or love. A good story will contextualize these peaches, deepen
your interest in them, explain why I wanted to create a painting
or essay to preserve them, and why, though ripe and sweet, they
were so hard to eat.

The story behind my still life begins with a walk. Even before
I took the first step of that walk, I knew that I would remember
it for the rest of my life.

On Friday, August 17, 2012, I drove the sixty miles between my home in Lincoln and the airport in Omaha with my daughter, Meredith, her violin, and her two enormous suitcases. She was catching a plane that morning to New York City where she would study violin as a graduate student at a music conservatory. Since her dream had always been to live in that wild and alluring city, I suspected that she'd remain there after she graduated. This was the day that I'd dreaded ever since I understood, really understood, that eventually she would leave not only our home but this part of the country.

Meredith and I arrived in Omaha earlier than expected. Rather than spend more time at the airport than we had to, we decided to walk. I parked behind an old, family-owned restaurant where she and I had eaten several times—thick homemade soups, brownies the size of shingles, and such a wide selection of pie (strawberry, sweet potato, pecan, sour cream raisin, banana cream, rhubarb, lemon meringue, chocolate, apple, peach) that I often had to ask someone to help me choose. On at least a few occasions, Meredith and I had walked in an old, hilly neighborhood north of the restaurant. It was a fitting place for her last walk in Nebraska as a Nebraska resident.

Just a few blocks from the restaurant we came upon a peach tree. The branches hanging over the backyard privacy fence were bent low with the weight of the fruit; golden peaches had fallen on the grass and sidewalk. How could anyone let such beautiful fruit go to waste? Some peaches were soft, bruised, or wormy, but most were unblemished and at or near their prime. We decided that on our way back to the car we'd gather some of the fruit that had fallen on the grass between the sidewalk and the curb.

As we walked those old hills, we chatted about the new lives that we were both entering, lives that would be filled more with others than with each other. We had cried on the drive to Omaha, heaping a soggy pile of Kleenexes on the floorboard as we confessed our fears about what lay ahead and our deep gratitude for each other. On the walk, Meredith sparkled with excitement about all the people she was going to meet, some of whom would offer opportunity, friendship, love; and we speculated about the mystifying interplay of genes, hard work, and chance that would decide her fate . . . and mine. I was certain that a bright and fulfilling personal and professional life awaited her. But because the voids created by the loss or absence of loved ones had become harder to fill as I've aged, I was less optimistic about my own prospects. My hopes for myself were minimal: I simply wanted to get through Meredith's departure and the hard days that followed without coming undone.

On the way back to the car, we stopped at the tree and gathered as many peaches as we could fit into the green baseball cap Meredith had worn on our walk, plus a few more that I carried. She set the fruit-filled cap on the floorboard of the passenger side of the car; then, before we went into the airport, she grabbed two of the peaches to eat in the air somewhere between Omaha and New York.

Once inside, we talked and laughed and wept. The biggest chunk of our talk was about my getting a haircut, a seemingly silly thing to concern ourselves with on such a momentous day, except that I'd worn a waist-length braid for decades and now I was wild to be gone with it. We talked about where I should get it cut and by whom, how much (not all of it, though a good nine inches), and why (Meredith's departure marked the end of one era and the beginning of a new one in my life, and I wanted to look as well as feel different). I became a little nauseous and giddy at the thought of walking into Iasan & Sebastian Salon with my braid and leaving without it.

We stood in the line for airport security until I was forbidden to go any farther with Meredith. When she emerged at the other end of the checkpoint, she turned, blew kisses, and disappeared. Because I expected this moment of physical separation to be devastating and didn't want to be in a crowded airport when it hit, I had planned to make a hurried exit. But instead of feeling grief-stricken or numb or flooded with love or pride or self-pity, I felt a surprising surge of lightness and joy. This wasn't the response I'd anticipated, and for a moment I felt guilty, but then I understood. For almost twenty-eight years I'd mothered my two children, putting them at or near the center of almost everything, and now the job was done . . . or, more likely, was becoming something else. But at that moment, I was nobody's mother. Life opened up before me in ways that delighted and then frightened me. Soon I would cut my hair, but beyond that I didn't know what I'd do with myself or how I'd live in the newly opened spaces.

When I returned to my car and opened the door, I smelled the peaches. Then I saw them in the bowl of the hat that Meredith had left behind, and for the first of what would be many times I remembered the peach tree, the hills north of the restaurant, our glimpses into the future, and how acutely aware I'd been on our walk of the passage of time . . . one minute less with Meredith at this stage of our lives . . . one minute less before the next stage began. After this tumble of images, I imagined entering my house, now absent of my daughter's presence but with signs of her everywhere—the sheets she'd slept on the past several nights; the towel she'd used to dry herself after her shower the night before; her coffee mug in the sink; her old sandals on the dining room floor; a note jotted on the back of a tea bag wrapper and left on the stove: "Call me. Back at 2:15." I felt a pang of . . . sadness? regret? yearning? Then the lightness and joy returned. I got in the car, picked out a couple of peaches to eat, and headed home.

Nothing in the still life on my kitchen counter suggests this story behind the peaches, my complicated feelings, or how sacramental it was to eat that fruit, as if I were taking my daughter's departure into my body with each delicious bite. For all the viewer knows, I bought the peaches at Super Saver for the purpose of arranging a still life, or I harvested them from a tree that grows in my backyard—there is no such tree, though I've long dreamed of having a small peach orchard—or the man that I'd been seeing for a couple of months before and several after Meredith's departure (and whose presence made her leaving easier to bear, a man who shared the bounty of his garden and orchard with me) brought those peaches and left them on the counter in a rather bell-shaped basket darkened with use, a basket so right for including in a still life. There's a story *there*, too: if the peaches he'd brought were the ones I'd chosen for my imagined still life and the subject of this essay, the story of his distracting, frustrating, yet enlivening presence would be primary and that of my daughter's departure secondary.

The uncracked wishbone from last Thanksgiving that teeters on the edge of the basket with the slightest disturbance also bears a story. When I asked Meredith to make a wish and pull, she refused. "You don't know what you're messing with when you wish on something," she said. Though I don't know how wishing, praying, cursing, or spell-casting work, I don't doubt their power. Since Meredith issued that warning, I haven't been able to pull the wishbone, nor can I throw it away.

Now that you know this story about her refusal to call forth a wish to enact the ritual with the physical object that would empower her intention, you might see the intact wishbone and its untapped potential as the focal point of the scene. You might, in fact, prefer that I call the scene "Still Life with a Wishbone" instead of "Still Life with Peaches." But I'm not ready to tell a story about the powers and dangers of wishing.

Finally, there's an old story about innocence and desire that this still life recalls for me. When I was a child, I thought that all peaches came from tin cans and looked either like goldfish or like turtles. I preferred the turtles, even though they scooted across my plate when I tried to cut them with a fork. Then, I didn't know that my enjoyment of eating uniformly golden-orange, skinless, syrupy slices and halves would be so different from the pleasure I'd one day receive when biting through the red and yellow skin of a fresh peach, velvety as a horse's muzzle . . . biting into the flesh, with its lovely mix of sweet and acid, pulling the last bits of peach meat from the husk, cracking the husk open, and holding the smooth tan seed on my tongue.

NEGATIVE SPACE

After Virginia Woolf heard her sister Vanessa Bell and their friend and art critic Roger Fry talk about *Les Pommes*, a Cezanne still life, she asked in her diary, "What can 6 apples *not* be?" That's easy. Six peaches. Yet, I wonder if Bell and Fry had so analyzed the placement and the lovely tonal harmonies of the apples in Cezanne's still life that what Woolf had posed was a question asking for more than an easy answer, more than analysis, more than words. Perhaps Woolf was thinking of the space between and around the apples that shapes, identifies, and balances. Like the space between words and musical notes, it's the silent, still place where the mind can rest.

BANISHMENT AND RETURN

I find still life paintings alluring and repelling, consoling and alienating. Take Alice Neel's *Still Life Spring Lake* (1969). On a table top in the lower center of the painting sit a brown lidless crockery jar and eight pieces of golden fruit—five to the viewer's right of the jar and three to the left. (Peaches? Apples? Pears? Golden plums? Apricots?—one could make a case for each.) You can see the entirety of the brown tabletop—a brown that contains patches of peach, green, and blue—and the cutlery drawer in the white table frame, but you can't see the legs. A curved, white, spoke-back chair facing the viewer is pushed in close to the table. In the distance you see the middle section of a narrow white refrigerator, and to the right the bottom of a wooden door painted a pale, chalky blue with recessed panels edged in gold. To the left of the refrigerator is an open doorway; beyond that are an orange floor and a cane-bottom chair pushed against a peach-colored wall. Because of the limited, downward-angled perspective, I feel as if I'm bending over to peer at this scene. I want to stand up and see what is closed off to me: the top of the refrigerator front, where there might be a recipe torn from a magazine or someone's to-do list held to it by magnets; the rest of the wooden door where there might be a pane of glass in the top half, through which I could see Spring Lake. I want to sit at the table, look into the brown crock and see what's within. (Cookies? Honey? Cobwebs? Pennies?) I want to check the golden fruit, touched with red and green, for ripeness. But nothing in this painting invites me to pull out the chair and sit down. Could I ever feel at home in such an unwelcoming place?

The attraction and repulsion I feel when viewing a still life speaks of the deep intentions of this genre. Art historian Norman Bryson, in his study of the eighteenth-century French painter Jean-Baptiste-Siméon Chardin, says that on one hand, still life establishes the subject "as a reality that is beyond all doubt and that occupies the position of centre with regard to everything else." On the other hand, "the things of the world"—the golden fruit, the brown crock, and the spoke-backed chair, things that we'd consider marginal or complementary if we saw them in a portrait—"appear as if they have no living bond with this watchful subject locked up inside the self." This rift between the beholder and the beheld explains the contradictory impulses I feel when I look at this painting: I find the scene in Neel's still life beautiful and desirable, and so I want to enter it, yet I find the scene in Neel's still life sealed off, not just to me but to all human life. Because there's a barrier that keeps me from entering the place where I'd like to be, I'm uneasy and want to look away.

Is the unsettling sense of exile I feel when viewing a still life owing to the purported absence of narrative or to the room seeming to have been emptied of narrative? The difference is crucial. *Absence* means that something is lacking or not present, perhaps never existed. To be *emptied* means that once something was there, but it has since been purged, erased, drained, deleted, ripped out, or carried away. I don't believe that a *complete* lack of narrative is possible. Depictions of ripe fruit, fruit that was once green and will soon spoil and rot, suggest a fundamental narrative. So I must qualify my use of these terms: narrative is *relatively* absent in a still life painting; the painting has been emptied of all but the subtlest of narratives.

In truth, a still life suggests a profound story about subject-object relationships. Bryson says that the genre not only addresses the experience of the solitary, isolated subject gazing out at an objectified field from which he or she has been removed or barred entrance, but it also addresses the subject as one who is part of "a vast preceding cultural community," and so is far from alone. The awareness that a single viewer is one of the countless many who have seen peaches as a source of both of sustenance and beauty redefines the subject-object relationship and, according to Bryson, *pulls* the cold, objectified outer world back toward the subject. However, I discern a different return movement. When I take the place not of a solitary, isolated beholder but as part of the multitude gathered before a still life painting, the scene from which I had been exiled *beckons* me to enter it. That, to my mind, is the allure of still life.

"Banishment" and "return" is what Bryson calls this movement, which resonates for me because the dominant story in my life has been that of seeking and creating hearth and home, of *being at home*—and now that my son and daughter have made their own homes, I feel I've lost or relinquished so much of what I once considered essential.

Questions claim me: Should I try to return to home as I once knew it? Should I go in search of a new and different kind of home? Should I not only learn to be content with my homelessness but see it as a blessing and sell off my house, furniture, books, and china until I'm light enough that I can go where the wind or my whims carry me? Should I find home in other people's homes? Should I cultivate the ability to see home both everywhere and nowhere?

When I returned "home" from taking Meredith to the airport and her new life, I set the peaches on the counter and put her hat in the closet. Then I turned around and saw my living room, dining room, and kitchen as if for the first time. Even though I knew the history of the objects in these rooms and their significance to me, at that moment they were not my things and this was not my home. I might as well have just entered a train station in a foreign country.

The first time I felt exiled from my own home was over twenty-five years ago when my son, Ian, was two. One Sunday evening while we were playing at the park, I noticed that he was limping. The next day he refused to walk and had reverted to crawling. The next day, he was so feverish and listless that I stayed home from work so I could take him to the doctor. Over the next two days several doctors, including a surgeon, examined Ian. Blood tests and X-rays revealed that he had an infection in his left thigh bone, an old-fashioned disease from which people used to die or lose limbs or become permanently crippled. Ian's was the first case of osteomyelitis in a child that any of the medical staff at Iowa Lutheran Hospital had ever seen.

Once Ian was in the care of the pediatric nurses at the hospital, I drove to my rented duplex in south Des Moines to take a shower and pack some food and clothes. When I walked into my living room, I was stunned by what I saw: my son's blue pajamas where I'd left them after I'd dressed him that morning; the rocking chair with a blanket draped over the arm because I'd held and rocked him before we left; his toys where he'd last played with them, including a fire truck near the front door and an orange crayon near the television. So much in my life that I thought was stable had been overthrown that day by the gravity of his illness. Yet here were our objects, just where we had left them. They had been his, mine, ours—and now they weren't ours because their familiar everydayness was gone. I felt spit out by the stillness, left broken and forsaken in a room I barely recognized. I realized that if my son died, I could not continue living in this scene, in this duplex, in this neighborhood, in this city, where I'd be reminded of his presence and absence by such common details as my old rocking chair and every orange crayon. I could not reclaim these objects I had known from before the split that occurred that day because to do so would have meant ignoring or denying what we'd been through—the surgeon's initial hunch that a tumor was the problem, learning of the extent of the damage to the femur and the likelihood of surgeries in the future to correct it, my musings about life without Ian and about who I'd be if I were no longer his mother.

I decided that if Ian never came home again, I'd quit my high school teaching position and move to Madison, Wisconsin, or Albuquerque, New Mexico, to some pleasant place that had no connection to Ian. There, I would pursue a PhD in English at the local university so that I could learn to write essays and teach adults. Or perhaps I'd enroll in a vocational school and learn the locksmithing trade, so I could work for myself instead of someone else and because I loved the metaphors associated with locks and keys. I'd make new friends and learn new things in my efforts to fill in or at least cordon off the treacherous hole in my life that Ian's absence would create.

At first, I found this progression in my thinking disturbing. How could I stand here and calmly plan a life without my son? But then I found it restorative, in part because it demanded that I be exquisitely aware of how much he meant to me and of the ways his presence had changed me, something I seldom thought about as I rushed around in the morning getting him ready for the babysitter and myself for work, or as I crammed in as much paper grading, grocery shopping, class preparation, laundry, houseclearing, and "quality time" with Ian as I could on the weekends. Being restored in that way made me able to become present again to my living room, to my home, and to my life in this place.

After experiencing this different kind of movement—from banishment to return—caused by my view of the seemingly abandoned objects in my living room, I was still: *still* as in "not moving," "free of sound," or "free from disturbance"; and *still* as in "yet," "more," or "nevertheless."

Still life. Calm, quiet, and motionless, yet alive and ripe with possibilities.

After two weeks in the hospital and six weeks with nurses who came to our home or the babysitter's home every six hours to inject strong antibiotics through a tube surgically implanted into Ian's chest, the bone infection was gone and his recovery complete. At some point, I slipped back into the everyday vision of my living room, paying attention to the toys, furnishings, books, plants, and knickknacks only when I needed them.

Likewise, now that Meredith and I have found ways to stay deeply, closely in touch through frequent telephone calls and my visits to her home in New York City, I rarely notice the basket, wishbone, and incense burner on my kitchen counter, or consider that my counter once held peaches we gathered on an unforgettable walk, or dwell on that final reconciling act of consuming the peaches.

Next year at this time, there will be peaches on my counter—of that I am sure—but I don't know where they will come from, whether they will be sweet or tart, whether I will find them worthy of a still life, or what reflections they may provoke. Other losses or the anticipation of losses will beckon me to reenact the story of banishment and return.

~~~~~~

While I ate the peaches that Meredith and I had gathered, I did so with sadness and regret because, as I consumed each one, I realized I was further and further from the day when I had gathered them with my soon-to-be-leaving, on-the-brink-of-so-much daughter. But I also ate them with pleasure—golden, fragrant, and sweet.

Living Parables

After the last session of the morning at the environmental literature conference, I drove downtown to buy lunch. I knew my way around that part of Lawrence, Kansas. A few years earlier my daughter and I had passed two days in this university town of about 90,000 people on the Kansas River while a luthier repaired her violin. She and I had walked along the river, browsed in the boutiques, visited what may have been the best local history museum I've ever seen, and dined at two good restaurants, one Thai, one Indian. If I found either, I'd order a take-out meal and eat in one of the downtown parks.

Massachusetts, the main street in Lawrence's vibrant downtown, is lined with shops, eateries, galleries, theaters, bars, and offices, and none of the empty or boarded up buildings that I see in too many Midwestern downtowns. Even though classes weren't in session at the University of Kansas on this last day of May, there was a steady flow of people on the sidewalks and not enough parking spaces for those in the slow-moving traffic. I had driven south, almost to the end of the strip, the part of Massachusetts Street that ran from Sixth to Twelfth Streets, when a pickup truck pulled out of the first parking space next to the cross walk. I whipped my car into the slot. Forty minutes of time remained on the meter—enough. I checked my visitor's guide to Lawrence. Zen Zero was a couple of blocks north on Massachusetts Street; the India Palace was on Tenth Street, just one block from where I'd parked. Hmmm. Thai peanut sauce or something with curry and garam masala?

Twenty minutes later, I emerged from the India Palace carrying a bag with two containers, one of rice and one of aloo kurma. I was so hungry that I planned to wolf down a few bites as soon as I got in my car, then drive to Watson Park and savor the rest of my meal there. I turned at the intersection and walked north on Massachusetts. My car wasn't in the corner space where I thought I'd left it, so I kept walking. Outside of a little boutique with a propped-open front door, a whiteboard sign announced that high-waisted shorts, long dresses, and flat sandals were the "hot" summer fashion items of 2013. Staying "cool" was my summer fashion goal, so I would not be adding any long dresses to my wardrobe. But maybe I'd stop by later to look at the high-waisted shorts. At the end of the block, I saw my blue, two-door Honda Civic waiting for me near the crosswalk. Apparently, the walk from my car to the restaurant had been a greater distance than I remembered. Just as I was about to unlock the door, I noticed that the cloth bag on the backseat wasn't mine. Nor did I have Mardi Gras beads hanging from the front mirror. I was embarrassed and hoped that no one had seen me try to enter a car that wasn't mine.

I continued walking north. I was sure that the distance from my car to the restaurant hadn't been this great. But it's easy to get turned around when you're in a place you're barely familiar with. I figured that after having spent the morning sitting through panel discussions devoted to climate change–induced migrations, indigenous environmentalism, bio-political disasters, and postcolonial ecocriticism, I was a little disoriented and mildly depressed. So I wasn't surprised that I'd forgotten where I'd parked my rubber-burning, petroleum-swilling car, assembled by underpaid workers in some faraway place.

The sky was clear, and everything looked washed clean after the heavy rains of the night before. It felt good to be out walking. A young man with hemp-colored dreadlocks sat at a table outside of Chipotle, devouring a burrito. A rangy, leather-skinned man slouching on a bench strummed a guitar. Though I couldn't tell what he was playing, I found the cords pleasant enough that I stopped to listen for a few minutes. An elderly couple in Birkenstocks and thick socks strolled past while holding hands. Three aggressively chipper teenagers were offering free samples of frozen yogurt in tiny paper cups that most people were refusing. I noted the presence of two frozen yogurt shops, one on each side of the street. If I ate all my rice and aloo kurma, frozen yogurt and a heap of berries might be enough for my evening meal.

At Seventh and Massachusetts Streets, one block short of the north end of the strip, I stopped. Where on earth was my car? Not here. I turned around and headed back the way I'd come. This time, I paid more attention to the cars than to the people, signs, and shops. By the time I reached Massachusetts and Tenth, not far from the India Palace, I still hadn't found my car, and I was worried. Downtown Lawrence isn't that big. Even if I had forgotten where I'd parked my car, I should have found it by now. What was going on? "Please, God," I prayed. "Help me find my car." Revision. "Please, God. Help me find my car and stay calm." I turned around and walked from Tenth to Seventh Street again, this time noticing every small, blue vehicle—the Prius (not mine); the Honda Fit EV (not mine); the Toyota Corolla (not mine); the Hyundai Accent (not mine). So many little blue cars The forty minutes of paid time remaining on the meter where I'd left my car had surely expired by now. I wouldn't be surprised to see a parking ticket clamped beneath my windshield wiper—if I ever saw my car again. Parking spaces *were* at a premium. But would the City of Lawrence have towed my car already? I could call the police and ask about this. But I supposed that at some point during the conversation, I'd have to admit to losing my car. Such an admission might make me look scatterbrained or addled. "You say that you're here attending a conference. Can you tell me where it's being held?" the officer might ask.

When I reached Tenth and Massachusetts, I turned and walked the six-block loop yet again. Maybe I should ask someone for help. People on the street might be in a hurry to get to their appointments or their lunch dates and brush me off. But an idle clerk wouldn't be giving up free time. An ample, thirty-something woman carrying a watering can stepped out of a shop to water the geraniums. She not only knew that long dresses and flat sandals were in but was confident enough to wear bold horizontal stripes over her generous bosom and hips. She looked friendly and like the type of person who could take control of a situation. Perhaps I could ask her for help. But really, what could she do? Drive me up and down Massachusetts Street while I searched for my car? I could contact one of the people I knew who was attending the conference. But forgetting where one parked one's car was an early symptom of dementia. They'd probably ask me if I knew the name of the current president of the United States. I would not be telling any of my professional friends about my predicament.

It's in situations like this that I realize how much I dislike traveling alone. Part of the reason for this is that since 2005, I've commuted over 100 miles roundtrip two or three times a week during the fall and spring semesters between my home in Lincoln and my job at the University of Nebraska–Omaha. I've grown weary of all that I've had to negotiate—keeping my car in tip-top condition for the commute, rough weather, inattentive drivers, stalled or backed up traffic, my own boredom or drowsiness, and the worst: living a life that is split between two cities. What I've come to dread while traveling alone on longer trips to farther places are car breakdowns, the oppressive loneliness that I feel in motel rooms, the dilemma of whether to eat alone in a restaurant, which makes me feel even lonelier and far too conspicuous, or to destroy more of the ozone layer with a polystyrene take-out box and plastic utensils. And then there were the unusual hitches like this one, of misplacing my car.

Before I became a commuter, I craved leaving the city and experiencing the unfamiliar, so I took a road trip about once a month. But after I became a commuter, I traveled beyond Lincoln and Omaha only when I had to—to see my daughter in New York City or my mother in rural Ohio; to attend a conference once a year or so; occasional trips to other cities or towns to give readings at bookstores, libraries, and art galleries. I count it a loss that the movement through geographical space that my commuting requires has dampened my appetite for the uncertainties and epiphanies of true travel, of "launching oneself into the unknown," as travel writer Paul Theroux describes it.

As I walked briskly up Massachusetts Street for the third time, I looked not at people or cars but for Nebraska license plates, a meadowlark on the left, a wand of goldenrod on the right against a gray-white background. Apparently, there was no one from Nebraska in downtown Lawrence, Kansas, on that day. Perhaps I was the butt of some surreal prank or anti-Cornhusker sentiments that involved moving my car or causing it to dematerialize. Or was the City of Lawrence like the Land of Oz, a place that I could leave only if I found and activated my latent powers? In the absence of a powerful good witch or a pair of magical slippers, home would remain but a hope and a memory.

I was so hungry that I was a shaky—or perhaps the shakiness was due to panic. I decided that when I reached the north end of my loop, I'd walk the few blocks to the park and eat my lunch. Once refreshed, I'd return to my search. If I still couldn't find my car, I'd humble myself and ask for help.

Watson Park was damp from the heavy rains of the night before. But I found a relatively dry bench and plunked myself down. I lifted the aloo kurma out of the bag and opened the flaps on the box. When the tantalizing aroma hit my nose, I shut my eyes in pleasure. Just seeing the chunks of potatoes, my number one comfort food, floating in the orange-brown gravy made my mouth water. I reached in the bag for a fork and napkins, but the bag was empty! I had silverware and napkins in my car, but what good was that now? I should have ordered finger food—a burrito or sandwich. Or I should have checked the bag for plastic cutlery before I left the restaurant. I returned to the loop on the verge of tears. The bag of food seemed heavier, as if it was filled with bricks. And I was so hungry.

Again, I trudged down Massachusetts Street even though I knew that the search was futile. When I reached Tenth and Massachusetts, I stopped. What if I never found my car? At the time, it didn't occur to me that there were simple solutions to my problems. I could have gotten my dopamine rush by eating the potato chunks with my fingers and then washed up at the park water fountain. I could have waited until shops on Massachusetts closed and most of the parked cars were gone. Then I could have more easily found my car. To pass the time, I could have hung out with the guitar player or toured the historical society museum or napped on a park bench or eaten frozen yogurt heaped with toppings in one of the two perky froyo shops.

I simply had to overcome my pride and fear and ask for help. "Please show me who to ask," I prayed. As I stood there waiting for an answer, it occurred to me that there was yet another block of the strip between Tenth and Eleventh Streets that hadn't been part of my loop. Even though I didn't remember parking that far south, I crossed the street. And there it was: my little blue car, only forty feet beyond the point where I'd turned around again and again and again. I was as delighted as the woman in the Biblical parable who lit a lamp, swept her house, and searched until she found her missing coin. But, too, I was confounded. Each time I'd walked my loop, I had stopped a little short of finding what I was looking for. My loop. I had been like a dog, running the same path back and forth next to the fence, wearing a deep rut into the earth. Or perhaps I was more like a rat obsessively running the same path leading to the same dead ends in a laboratory maze.

The parking meter had expired, but there was no ticket tucked beneath the windshield wiper. I slipped into the driver's seat. Oh, had I missed my car! The first afternoon session of the conference would start soon. There were two papers that I wanted to hear,

"Dormancy: Learning the Patience of Plants with Jean-Loup Tras-sard" and "Environmental Justice and the Toxic Sublime," that were being presented at the same time in different sessions. I'd make a better decision about which to attend on a full stomach. I took a plastic fork and a napkin from the glove compartment and ate.

That evening, I recounted my adventure to my daughter by telephone. What I wanted and needed was just a little beyond where I was looking. "It was as if I was in a living parable," I told her.

~~~~~

Parables trap us.

Etymology teaches how this entrapment occurs. The term parable comes from the Greek word *parabolè* which is comprised of the root *bole*, which means "to throw," and the preposition *parà*, which means "the other side." Literally, *parabole* means to "throw along" or "put side by side" and has come to mean "similitude," "comparison," or "metaphor." In *Teaching Through Parables: Following Jesus*, Robert D. Badenas writes that a *parabolè*, like a *parabola* in geometry, "is the indirect, curved trajectory of a projectile going from point A to point B over an obstacle." We turn to parables to teach hard truths because, says Sallie McFague, a Christian theologian who has written extensively about the form, "difficult, strange, unfamiliar matters must be approached with the utmost cunning, imagination, and indirection in order for them to be seen at all." The parable achieves this through its curved trajectory. Badenas says that as a rhetorical device, a parable is a "narrative that allows the storyteller to reach the intended target through an unexpected itinerary or path, so that the receiver cannot prevent the result and avoid the impact."

At the heart of a good parable is the shock or surprise that violates our conventional view of the world: all the laborers in the vineyard are paid the same wages, whether they worked one hour or a full day; those who take the lowest seats at the banquet will be given the seats of greatest honor in God's Kingdom; the shepherd will leave ninety-nine sheep untended so he can search for the lost one. While sitting among the pigs he tended in a country far from home, the "lost" or "prodigal" son "came to his senses" (NIV) or "came to himself." (NKJ) Nothing in the parable tells or even suggests exactly how or why this happens, though we know that epiphany and transformation are more likely to strike when one is in dire straits or down and out than when one is reaping a good harvest or seated where one expects to be at or near the head of the banquet table. Or when your car is exactly where you remember leaving it and the take-out food comes with cutlery and plenty of napkins.

Theologian Paul Ricoeur says that parables exhibit "a pattern of orientation, disorientation, and reorientation." Where the realism breaks down, one finds a reversal of expectations and for a moment, says McFague, the "participant" (i.e., the listener or reader) loses control. That is also the point where the meaning lies. What most disorients in the parable of the lost or prodigal son is the younger son's audacious request for his portion of his inheritance from his still living father and the father's lavish and loving response when that son returns home after having burned through his money and living in a shameful manner. At this point, the reader or listener experiences the *reorientation*, the change of focus or direction, the adjustment or realignment that follows disorientation, that Ricoeur identifies as central to the parable. Where the parable catches us off guard is where it traps us and leads, coaxes, forces us to see new possibilities. Through this parable, Jesus suggests that such extraordinary and illogical generosity and forgiveness are traits of God and God's kingdom.

Reading or hearing parables as extended metaphors provides an open space where we can imagine ourselves into the lives of each of the characters and test other ways of thinking and living. This enlarges our capacity for understanding other people's beliefs and desires, which in turn, expands our ability to communicate with and understand them. But, too, parables crack *us* open, shake us up, break up the hard ground so that the tiniest mustard seed of what we most need to develop—wisdom, compassion, discernment, humility, wholeness, generosity, love—can take root and sprout, eventually becoming the largest tree in the garden. This provides an opportunity for us to touch some awkward, troublesome, or terrible truth we might otherwise avoid through denial or intellectualization. I've been reading and thinking about the parable of the Lost Son, a story of fewer than 700 words, for many decades and marvel that I continue to discover new meanings in it. I've been the rude, ungrateful, lost child; I've been the rejoicing parent who has welcomed home the lost child who broke my heart; I've been the resentful, judgmental older sibling who refuses to celebrate the success or return of another, and so is even more "lost" than one who once ate and slept with pigs. Like the father, I've modified or broken seemingly hard-and-fast rules or laws in favor of love. Shortly after I had lost and found my car, I realized that that experience is asking me what it means for one at my stage in life to leave home for a far country. Would I ever return? Would there even be a home for me to return to? If so, what boon would I bring to share with others? If I didn't return home, would I live in despair and regret? Freedom and joy? Would I continue roaming? Would I create a new home? Or, could I make new the home in which I've long lived?

~~~~~

Parabling is a way of conceiving of and framing our experiences. I may have first grasped this when a woman at a church I belonged to many years ago told the half dozen or so of us with whom she was sharing a table at fellowship time an autobiographical story in which I recognized the curved trajectory and the potentially disruptive and life-altering properties of the parable.

What we listeners already knew was that twenty-five years earlier, when this woman was in her mid-twenties, she survived a bad car crash that required many months of intense medical care. Her husband, put off by the changes in her appearance and mobility and the long, demanding recovery ahead of her, divorced her. Though the woman recovered, she was never able to hold a job, had a pronounced limp, and a damaged facial nerve that had immobilized part of her face. Since the accident, she had lived on social security disability insurance, which meant that she lived near the poverty line. She'd never remarried and this woman, who was smart, educated, interesting, and committed to social action, probably hadn't had a date in decades. When I walked the trail around Campus Lake, I'd sometimes see her, dragging her weak leg. When she saw me, she'd give me her half smile, and we'd chat a bit. Her parabolic story goes something like this:

A woman was walking on the path around the lake, just as she had every morning for many years, when she saw a robust man with luxuriant white hair approaching her from the opposite direction. "You're walking the wrong way," he said to her. "You're right," she said. She turned around and walked—with him. The man confessed that he had spoken to the woman with such boldness because he found her so beautiful. Within weeks, they married.

Some of us who heard this tale admired the man for speaking so forwardly to the woman. Others found the man's remark to a stranger, "You're walking in the wrong direction," as if there was a right one, brash and presumptuous. They found the woman's response, a sudden, willing, and complete surrender to his request, worrisome. But some insisted that that wasn't how she understood the man's comment. In fact, what *she* heard was an invitation to change her life for the better, which she accepted. But even those who heard a warning in the story suggesting that this man might be domineering and judgmental, were surprised, amazed, and delighted at what can happen when people open their hearts and minds and take a risk. This "Parable of the Sudden Reversal" asks us what miracles, invitations, and cautions await those of us with the eyes to see and the ears to hear as we travel our well-worn paths.

To craft my parable about losing and finding my car, I followed the formula offered by Alyce McKenzie, Professor of Homiletics at SMU's Perkins School of Theology. She says that the parable form contains "something realistic, something strange, something within view, and something out of range." This allows the author to capture the parabolic movement of reaching the target through a less than direct path so that, as Badenas said, "the receiver cannot prevent the result and avoid impact." I pare my story down to the nub; I cast myself as a character who I speak of in the third person, a distance that permits self-scrutiny, and something of the otherworldliness of a fairy tale. Through this pithy story, I show how I was trapped, ambushed, beguiled, baited, inveigled, and caught by the experience of losing and finding, and how that experience raised essential questions for me to answer. That is the magic of parabling.

THE PARABLE OF THE LOST AND FOUND CAR

A solitary traveler was hungry, so she went to the marketplace to buy food in the foreign land to which she had journeyed. After she got her food, she returned to the spot where she thought she'd left her car only to find that it wasn't there. She walked up and down the street, diligently searching. But she didn't see her car anywhere; her pride and fear kept her from asking for help.

When the woman reached her starting point yet again after many hours of searching, she gave up. She asked God to show her who to ask for help. At that moment, she lifted her eyes and there, just across the street, just yards from the point where she kept turning around on her search, she saw her car. "Oh, my little lost one," she exclaimed. "I've found you." She unlocked her car, got in, ate her food, and continued on her way.

It wasn't until I rewrote the story of my experience as a parable almost a decade after it happened that I saw what it might be pointing to a different meaning than that which I'd originally extracted from it. If every part of the parable is part of me, then the Parable of the Lost and Found Car asks me to think deeply about what part of myself I've lost or misplaced or never allowed to develop in the first place. Is that part of me now demanding a reckoning by insisting that I come and find it? Should I get into the habit of lifting my eyes and asking for help?

Yes, the parable answers. And, yes.

Daily Bread

I close the blinds, so I won't be distracted by the sight of cardinals in the forsythia bushes. I light a candle on the dining room table, place a slice of homemade bread on a china dessert plate, pour a glass of water, and sit down. I'm taking this bread straight—no cream cheese, no peanut butter, no jelly, no hummus. When I eat meals alone, which now is most of the time, I often skim the newspaper, scroll through Facebook posts, or listen to National Public Radio. What results is fast, distracted eating. What I am doing here, each mid-morning for ten minutes, is the opposite of that: eating with full and unflinching attention.

Since I was fifteen, I've limited my choices to two: bingeing on bread or abstaining from bread. Because the third choice, eating bread in moderation, is one with which I have had little experience, I fear that if I bring bread into my home, I might eat mindlessly or begin restricting again. Eating in moderation makes me nervous. Yet this choice is one of healing, since it means walking the narrow way that passes between the dichotomies of body and mind, flesh and spirit, control and surrender, bread as physical reality and bread as symbol. Christian theologian Marcus Borg refers to the narrow way as "the path of centering in the sacred." I hope that by enacting a ritual that involves making and eating bread that is at once physical and spiritual food, I will be nourished, filled, and healed.

When I was fifteen, I'd slip into the kitchen, either at home or in the homes of the families I babysat for, and find the softest, moistest loaf of factory-made white bread. I'd take two plain slices at a time, fold and scrunch them so that they were more condensed and eat. During my binges, it wasn't the taste or the nourishment of the bread that I was after but the soothing rhythm of filling my mouth, chewing, swallowing, and filling, again and again, and the way in which this ceremony seemed to fill the gaps and hollows within me, and to soften and blur everything around me. As I ate, secretively, ritualistically, alone, I was outside of myself, my mind no longer chewing on itself. Afterward, I felt sick from the bulk, the chemical additives, and my self-disgust. My weight soared; stretch marks appeared on my thighs.

The summer before my junior year of high school, I stopped eating bread and just about everything else except for precisely measured servings of fresh fruit, cooked vegetables, puffed rice cereal, and an occasional boiled egg, never more than 600 calories in one day. In the early 1970s, I had never heard of anorexia nervosa, nor had anyone I knew, including the pediatrician that my mother eventually took me to see because I was worried about my hair loss and curious about my amenorrhea ("You need to eat more," was his only advice). What I did know was that self-starvation seemed to offer the antidote to my belief that in so many ways, I wasn't good enough to win anyone's approval, including my own. But when I ate my tiny meals and rode my bike until I was exhausted, I was finally doing something better than anyone else. A few weeks into my austerities, I experienced a subconscious "click" and shifted into a new, higher gear. Then, I felt even more empowered to deny my appetite and, in turn, I became empowered by this denial. I may not have been conscious of the click and the shift at the time, but because I heard it and felt it during the other two periods in my life when eating very little became so easy and gratifying, I suspect that it happened then, too. Without the click and the shift, dieting requires an iron will. But in that higher gear, dieting is a piece of cake—or rather, it's as easy as gobbling a slab of my favorite rich yellow cake with thick, slick swirls of chocolate frosting. My austerities were so consuming that I had little time, energy, or attention for anything else. Since my mother was away during my time of austerities and my father, if he noticed them, said nothing, there was no one to interfere. By summer's end, I was thin, anemic, isolated, and triumphant.

~~~~

At the dining room table, I center myself by feeling my feet on the floor, my buttocks on the seat of the chair, and the small of my back firm against the back of the chair. I soften my breathing, my gaze, and the muscles in my face. I feel my hunger in my stomach, mouth, and brain. In my mind's eye, I see myself: a small, thin woman, with blue-green eyes, blond hair (though my face is framed by short, wiry gray hairs), a face that is longer than it used to be and etched with both laugh and frown lines, a body still supple from over thirty years of yoga practice. I see the dense, brown slice of bread that I will soon take into myself, one slow, deliberate, savoring bite at a time. This is not an ordinary meal but a homeopathic remedy, a strength-building regimen, a spiritual discipline, and a sacred rite.

~~~~

When I was twenty-five, the click and the shift and the restricting that followed it happened again, though not in the same way as when I was fifteen. As a new and underprepared high school teacher—a job, I soon discovered, with which I was temperamentally mismatched, far from home in a big city where I knew no one and feared everything it seemed—I came to believe that someone was tainting or poisoning my food. To protect myself, I hid food in my clothes closet, declined any food that I hadn't made with my own hands, threw out the food in my refrigerator and cupboards that seemed suspicious, and denied myself the communion meal at the Lutheran Church I frequented. The less I ate and the smaller I became, the more powerful I felt. Healing began two years later, when pregnancy and lactation stoked the fires of my appetite. Caring for a child who I loved so much that it frightened me shifted my attention away from my emptiness to his well-being. And I started writing and praying.

Three years into menopause, I heard the click and felt the shift again, though the restricting that followed was different. At fifty-four, I whittled down the list of foods that I could eat until it fit on my thumbnail and my weight dropped to a number that I hadn't seen since seventh grade. But this was a necessary austerity, I argued—a worsening of my food allergies and gastro-intestinal problems, and an intensification of my concerns about all those pesticides in the food supply, all those dangers lurking in foods made from genetically modified crops. By severely restricting what I ate, I was keeping myself healthy and safe. But deep down, I knew that as with the two earlier episodes of what I call my "malady," what I really wanted was to become a waif, a whisper, a flicker, a shadow.

It didn't occur to me that something was amiss until my twenty-year-old daughter told me that I had an eating disorder and that if I didn't start eating more, I'd die. Her words flicked on the light in a dark room. I was shocked by what I saw. For the past couple of decades, I'd rested comfortably on the line between normal and overweight, my face and saddlebags full, my bones hidden beneath flesh. But after my malady returned, my clavicles grew prominent; each shoulder became capped by a bony point. My ribs, visible from my armpits to my waist and from my clavicle to my sternum, reminded me of a washboard. My breasts, always small, were even tinier, and both the grape-sized lumps and the gritty little knots on the outer sides which I'd been able to find only with my fingertips, I could now see in the mirror. A pair of bony crests extended from either side of my lower abdomen.

When I looked over my shoulder, I saw a string of knobs, my spine. Prominent veins stood out on my arms and abdomen. My thighs no longer touched; my calves, always so fleshy that it was all but impossible for me to find boots that fit, now seemed normal sized, which made my knees look larger. My face had slackened and become more furrowed than it had before the return of my malady.

In response, I did what I always do when I don't understand what is happening to me: I researched. I was surprised to learn that about ten percent of those with eating disorders are older women. But, says Dr. Cynthia Bulik, the director of the Center of Excellence for Eating Disorders at the University of North Carolina, the percentage is most likely higher since most older women with eating disorders disguise or misread their symptoms as being due to a health condition, food sensitivities, or changes associated with aging, and so they aren't included in the number of reported eating disorders. In a 2012 study, Bulik and her research team found that women over fifty are engaged in unhealthy eating behaviors and thinking to the same extent that adolescents are. Now, more older women than ever before are seeking treatment for their eating disorders—a psychological illness and a clinical diagnosis—and disordered eating—an abnormal or maladaptive relationship with food, weight, and body image. Though at times, I have met the shifting "qualifications" for anorexia nervosa, I've never been diagnosed with it or treated by a specialist—not an uncommon position, I've discovered, for "restrictors" of all ages.

Eating disorders and disordered eating in older women differ from those found in girls and young women in several ways. First, we're more likely to restrict than to binge and purge. (I don't purge; it's been many years since I last binged or even splurged, say, on a pat of butter or a piece of cake.) Second, in their study of women who developed eating disorders after the age of forty, Dr. Edward Cumella and Zina Kally discovered that while adolescent female inpatients with eating disorders score high on the Eating Disorder

Inventory on "the drive for thinness, bulimia, and body dissatisfaction measures," older female inpatients with eating disorders
score higher on the "ineffectiveness, perfectionism, interpersonal
distrust, and asceticism [self-discipline] scales." We older women
care about our jiggly thighs and pouchy bellies, but not to the same
extent as our teenaged counterparts do. Apparently what matters
more to us than body image is meeting the unrealistically high
standards that we set for ourselves. Third, most experts that I've
read see a link between loss, grief, and depression and the onset
or return of an eating disorder in women who are middle-aged
or older. Clearly, my midlife restricting was about far more than
a desire to create a healthier lifestyle.

When Jesus saw an invalid of thirty-eight years waiting to be
healed by the Pool of Bethesda, he asked the question that cuts to
the heart of the matter, "Do you want to be made well?" Instead
of answering the question, the sick man told Jesus why he hadn't
been able to enter the healing waters. Apparently, he couldn't see
or imagine that healing might come to him in a different form than
he'd always thought it would. Apparently, he was too comfortably
at home with his infirmity to truly desire wholeness. I suspect
that most of us with eating disorders and disordered eating, when
asked, "Do you want to be made well?" would either insist that
there was nothing wrong with us or reject the invitation. No,
we don't want to be made well because that would mean eating
more (or less), weighing more (or less), and feeling more. No, we
don't want to be made well because our food-related thoughts and
behaviors provide us with identity, power, security, and purpose.
By restricting or bingeing, we believe that we can defy the forces
that threaten to weaken or destroy us. Bulik likens the attitude
of those with eating disorders toward their own recovery to the
experience of driving a car with one foot on the accelerator and
one on the brake: "One half is ready to embark on the journey,

but the other is not ready to relinquish control." And so, rather than being still, centered, harmonious, and at peace, one shakes, rumbles, and burns a lot of fuel while going nowhere.

~~~~~

I watch myself take a bite of bread, too small to be a mouthful, and put the slice back on the plate. How many calories will I consume during this ritual? About eighty. Even though I'm remarkably accurate when estimating the number of calories in a serving of food, I'm anxious and my stomach is full of needles. How careless of me not to have tallied the total number of calories in the entire loaf when I made it, measured the length of the loaf before I sliced it and the thickness of the slice on my plate, and then divided the width of the slice into the length of the whole so I'd know the exact number. Seventy-eight? Eighty-two? There's a difference, you know. I start to run the numbers in my head (one-third of a cup of oil, 630 calories, two packets of dry yeast, 42 calories . . .). Stop! Feet. Buttocks. Small of the back. Breath. Gaze. Hunger. This slice of bread.

~~~~~

On Palm Sunday when I was eleven, I was confirmed at Grace United Methodist Church in Burlington, Iowa. Later that week, on Maundy Thursday, I took communion for the first time. It was special going to church in the evening and seeing our beautiful, old sanctuary dimly lit. I was almost moved to tears by the solemnity and symbolism of the words and movements of our tall, black-robed pastor, the guy who wore pullover sweaters and joked with us at Saturday morning confirmation class, as he reenacted the Last Supper. During the communion, he held up a loaf of bread and broke it, repeating Jesus's words: "This is my body given for you; do this in remembrance of me." At that moment, I was in the upper room with the disciples, watching a ritual that, like them, I didn't fully understand. The pastor invited the congregation to the communion rail in groups. As we knelt, he served each of us a sip of grape juice in a tiny glass and a morsel of white bread.

I've always loved this rite of symbolic, communal eating and the idea that any given thing can stand for more than itself. In fact, my first communion may have been when I fell in love with metaphor. The bread and juice were Jesus's flesh and blood. By eating and drinking this meal, I was taking Jesus into my body and soul. Communion offered a robust theological metaphor whose significance for me has grown with time. Now when I hold the communion bread on my tongue and let it dissolve, I am struck by the genius and the appropriateness of Jesus's presenting himself as something so common, so consumable, so essential, so nourishing as the bread made in first-century Palestine.

Yet no bread has ever been enough for me. If I had been present when Jesus fed the five thousand with two fish and five loaves or when he served his disciples living bread in the upper room, I might have refused the gift or eaten it all, my portion and everyone else's. I pray for a stronger faith. I pray for the experience of enough.

Self-forgiveness comes through a surprising channel: my continuing research on my malady. In the past few decades, a growing number of studies reveal that those with eating disorders and disordered eating can't trust their brains to tell them the truth about when and when not to eat. For instance, one study found that when people with anorexia severely restrict their caloric intake, their abnormally high levels of serotonin drop, and they report feeling calmer and less anxious. Another study indicates that because those with bulimia and anorexia have an abnormal response to the taste of food in the right anterior insula, a part of the brain involved in appetite regulation, they don't accurately recognize or perceive signals about their hunger or satiety. Another study suggests that increased activity in the dorsal striatum leads to "maladaptive food choices" among restrictors, meaning that they actually prefer the plain, dry rice cake over the heavy, redolent slice of cheesy pizza.

And, too, those with eating disorders don't know when to be anxious or frightened or demanding of themselves and when to let go. In a 2004 study, Dr. Walter H. Kaye and his research team found that two-thirds of the subjects in the eating disordered groups they studied had "one or more lifetime anxiety disorders." Most of the subjects reported that the onset of their anxiety, obsessive-compulsive disorder, or phobia had occurred during childhood, before the symptoms of their eating disorder manifested. Another study shows that perfectionism, expressed both through rigid thinking and dissatisfaction with one's body, is a "robust, discriminating characteristic" of anorexia and, like anxiety, is likely to be one of a cluster of characteristics that are determined by the interaction of one's genetic makeup and environmental influences.

Because I can't control my serotonin levels or the structural and functional alterations in my insula and frontal cortex and because my tendency towards uneasiness, apprehension, and perfectionism are, at least in part, inherited, aspects of my malady are beyond my control. I am relieved and consoled by the knowledge that my malady is due not to a weak character, as too many would have those of us with disordered eating believe, but the chemistry or hardwiring of my God-made brain. But, too, this knowledge leaves me feeling resigned and hopeless. If I can't control this, should I even hope to be free of it? My malady has come to represent to me a battle for ascendancy between my genetics and brain chemistry and my faith in a God, with whom all things are possible. Each morning when I partake of the bread-eating ritual, I cast my lot with the latter.

I offer thanksgiving for this bread and ask for presence of mind and God's protection. Eating this bread will satisfy some of my hungers. But others—the hunger for love, approval, a sense of belonging, autonomy, and aging in such a way that I feel vital and valuable to myself and others, in spite of the growing invisibility that accompanies female aging in our culture—are beyond the power of any physical food. I must remain clear as to which hungers I'm humbly attending to and which are left wanting, so I never again hide, forget, deny, or disguise them. I vow not to waste this slice of my fleeting life on what cannot fill me or that keeps me from pursuing what can.

In *The Beauty Myth: How Images of Beauty Are Used against Women*, Naomi Wolf connects the explosion and exponential growth of eating disorders in the sixties, seventies, and beyond to a backlash against the gains made by Western women during that time—gains such as access to higher education, birth control and abortion, legal protections against discrimination, wider career options, and opportunities for economic independence. "When women came en masse into male spheres," Wolf writes, "that pleasure [of 'women's natural fullness'] had to be overridden by an urgent social expedient that would make women's bodies into the prisons that their homes no longer were." All one had to do to quiet a woman with high aspirations was to lower the correct or healthy weight for a woman of her height and age one stone (fourteen pounds) below the average woman's natural weight, thus redefining her natural shape and size as too big. Thereafter, says Wolf, "a wave of self-hatred swept over First World women, a reactionary psychology was perfected, and a major industry [weight loss] was born." The woman or girl with anorexia may have begun her journey bold and defiant, but from the perspective of a male-centered society, she ended up as the "perfect woman . . . weak, sexless, and voiceless" and very obedient. I can attest that a woman whose focus has narrowed to the seven celery sticks and the tablespoon of fat-free Ranch dressing on her plate and the number on the scale is not a woman with the time or mental and physical energy to claim her power, speak her mind, live large, or love fully.

Even though I take issue with Wolf's simplistic view that eating disorders are caused by just one factor—the reaction of a patriarchal culture to women's growing freedoms, instead of the snarl of genetic, biochemical, familial, psychological, spiritual, and cultural factors that I see—I am nonetheless strengthened and empowered by her thinking. No, it's a rawer feeling than that. I feel fighting mad when I read Wolf's statement that during her anorexic year, "all the space I had for dreaming was taken up by food." How does one recover a lost year? she asks. "Who is obliged to make reparations to me for the thought abandoned, the energy never found, the explorations never considered? Who owes me for the year-long occupation of a mind at the time of its most urgent growth?" With this, Wolf has given me something clear-cut and specific to push against. I won't let my malady take anything else from me.

I found a remedy for my malady in what I call the "replacement theory," which I developed after reading Wolf's book. According to this theory, I can take the precious time and energy that I once wasted with thoughts of food, calories, proportions, weight, self-image, and my many flaws, fears, and failures, and put them toward something that will bear good fruit. For instance, I could become fluent in another language; learn to dance (salsa, line, buck, jazz); widen my circle of friends and be in closer touch with old friends, both those that are near and those that are far away; learn to grow, prepare, and prescribe herbs to help others heal from whatever afflicts them; and use my communication skills and faith in shalom, the biblical model of peace, wholeness, and justice, to make more visible the faces and forces that create or allow poverty to exist in this wealthiest of nations.

Before we can begin to fill our heart's desires, women must, as Wolf says, "liberate the occupied territories of our minds and energies." When my homeland is occupied, I have options: I can submit, leave, go into hiding, or take on the tyrant who captured or seized what was once free and mine. I'm leaning toward the last.

~~~~

After I swallow, I pause. Before the next bite, I again center myself. Feet. Buttocks. Small of the back. Breath. Gaze. Hunger. This slice of bread. I see myself sitting at my dining table. I see the years that have gathered in my face and bones. I see this table where my former husband and sister-in-law, my son and daughter and I used to eat, chat, argue, and laugh together, but that now is almost always empty. I see that the dining room, kitchen, and living room are quiet, still, just as I left them. If there's clutter on the coffee table, it's mine; if there's a towel drying in the bathroom, it's mine.

It is of no surprise to me that I began restricting again in 2011. For a year or two prior to the return of my malady, I was at times unbearably sad and felt that my life had no purpose. My son, then twenty-six, had, after several bumpy starts, moved on with his adult life. My daughter, then twenty, was preparing to audition for graduate schools in faraway places. The members of my birth family and some of my dearest friends lived far away; my father was dead. Because of the demands of working, writing, and single-parenting, I hadn't forged enough bonds with people outside of my family while my children were still at home. Dating was a waste of time, since some men I kept company with wanted to become exclusive at once, with marriage not far off, while others wanted me to be a good sport about sharing their time and attention with other women. I wasn't interested in a hasty marriage or a place in a harem.

I was fiercely alone and sad. Hope had evaporated, leaving behind a dry, salty residue. A nagging sense of pointlessness often weighted me. I'd awaken in the night with a ripe ache or with hard knots of grief that made it difficult for me to fall back asleep. Several times I said to myself that I simply could not or would not continue living this way.

I began looking for ways to fill the emptiness I felt not with hunger and restriction but with good fruit. I brought more people into my life, by strengthening my ties with old friends and by making new ones. I began volunteering my time and talents. After twenty-five years writing and publishing nature essays, a solitary pursuit as I practiced it, I abandoned the genre and began writing about human relationships and communities, art, God, and spirituality. I don't know if I'll ever be completely free of my malady, but I do know that as I fill my heart's desires, the power and pleasure I derived from restricting lessened, and the flare-ups have become shorter, milder, and less frequent.

~~~

My healing rite involves just one slice of bread and ten minutes of my life spent in the here and now halfway between breakfast and lunch. But I don't look forward to it. Many days, I stall. Then I'm both the rule breaker and the rule enforcer. Just let me grade three more essays or answer five more email messages or run a little errand or make a phone call or sort the recycling, I tell myself. Or, since I'm running late for my office hours, would it be okay if I ate the slice in four swift bites while standing at the sink? But I remain firm. What I hope is that my daily bread eating exercise will eventually release me from my rigid, restrictive thinking. What I'm certain of is that my daily rite keeps me honest and dependent on God.

~~~

Because the master narrative our culture imparts about aging is that midlife and beyond is a time of inexorable decline, marked by decay, deterioration, powerlessness, dependency, irrelevance, and obsolescence, what many women fear the most is becoming an old woman. In short, it's the fear of aging that is the trigger, ignition switch, or motivating force for eating disorders in older women. Ironically, by restricting or bingeing, one intensifies the wrinkles, the wizened features, the sagging, the heaviness, the health problems, and the self-absorption that make one appear older than she is.

I've long believed that as a writer whose work is published, read, and honored; as a professor whose students value my knowledge and experience; as the mother of a son and daughter, both of whom have grown up to be so charmingly unconventional, each in their own way; and as one who seeks to dwell with God and in God's word, I was immune not to aging but to the stigma of aging, and that I was strong enough to resist the decline-through-aging narrative, a story that is so pervasive and sticky that we can't help but absorb it and pass it on. Yet I wasn't that resilient. I dread entering the country of old age which, in spite of the cheerful assurances that sixty is the new forty, seventy the new fifty, begins at sixty in my mind—soon, for me. It's infuriating to know that it doesn't have to be this way. By restricting my food intake, I enjoy a sense of power and control at a time when I am told, directly and indirectly, that as an older woman I should be experiencing a loss of power and control. When I go to bed hungry or only eat foods from a narrow, and narrowing, list of possibilities or spend too many hours a day exercising or lie about having just eaten a gut-splittingly big meal so I don't have to take more than a small plate of fruit from the buffet, it's because I've got a fight on my hands—against my own attitudes and those of my culture about aging. At its core, my restricting is about the desire to rid myself of pain, frustration, and shame. But it's a protest, balm, and purification that cannot inspire me to live a richer, deeper life and it achieves nothing of real value.

Along with directing my time and energy toward activities that bear good fruit, my healing also involves seeking out or crafting life-supportive narratives about old age as a time of power, passion, wisdom, insight, and inner growth, the deep story that I find in the work and biographies of primatologist Jane Goodall; activists Angela Davis, Marian Wright Edelman, and Jimmy Carter; artists Maria Lassnig and Georgia O'Keeffe; yoga teacher

Vanda Scaravelli; actors Meryl Streep and Helen Mirren; writers May Swenson and Louise Erdrich, and other heroes, both famous and not. I believe that by crafting my own resistance narrative, one that presents me as a woman of power and purpose, and by telling that story to myself often enough, I'll embrace and live it.

~~~~

I take a bite of bread. It's not as sweet as I like, since I forgot to add honey to the ingredients. Yet it's not perfection I crave but fullness and wholeness. I swallow and feel the bread moving down my throat and into my stomach. I take a sip of water. Bread and water: the food of prisoners. Bread and water: the food of liberation. I pick up the slice, take another small bite, and put it back on the plate. I let the bread dissolve on my tongue just as I do at the Lord's Supper, so I can savor the sacrifice and the fulfillment. It's a razor's edge I walk. How tempting it is to wolf down this slice and the rest of the loaf. How tempting it is to throw it into the sink as if it's on fire, douse it with water, and then cram it down the garbage disposal. But I remain at my dining table, eating with deliberation this slice of bread.

With one remaining bite of bread before me, I pause. I am poised between the past and future, between stuff or starve, between what I'm told about myself and what I know to be true, between dwelling in the present and all that might deprive me of that peace and fullness. This act of eating with the entirety of my being feels decadent and indulgent. How many of these simple, mindful meals will it take to erase the vestiges of all those times when I denied my desire for bread or ate bread as a filler? How many of these simple, mindful meals will it take to provide the fullness and wholeness I crave?

When I've eaten the last crumb, I blow out the candle, set my plate and glass in the sink, and open the blinds. I'm relieved that the ritual is done for another day. And yet, the bread tasted good and for a moment here and there, I found pleasure in eating it.

Doves for Dinner

For a recent birthday of mine, Ian and his partner, Brandy, invited me to their home, a rented trailer house on a cattle farm just outside of Lincoln, Nebraska—land that's been in the landlord's family since the days of the homesteaders. Brandy promised me a carrot cake with cream cheese frosting, a combination I love. Ian promised spring rolls with plenty of options that would appeal to me, a wide array of sauces from the Asian market, and butternut squash soup. But as with most meals at Ian and Brandy's, there was also a surprise on the menu.

When I arrived, Ian was on his shady porch, bending over a tray heaped with something gray and tan; his German shorthair, Duke, was sprawled near his feet and panting in the early September heat. As I drew closer, I saw Ian lift a limp, feathered corpse from the mound and snip off the black-spotted wings that had once whistled in flight; this allowed him to easily peel back the skin and feathers on the breast. He then jabbed his thumb beneath the V-shaped breastbone and his forefinger into the cavity beneath the throat, pulling the breast free of the body. Placing the glistening, purple-red muscle into a bowl with all the other muscles, each similar in size and shape to a large strawberry, he tossed the head, back, wings, entrails, and feet into a bucket.

Beautiful, gentle mourning doves—"rain crows," my great-grandmother had called them—are one of my favorite backyard birds. For me, their throbbing, plaintive coos are the sound of summer.

"Are the doves for dinner?" I asked.

I don't flinch when I see what my son is serving for dinner or ask questions about where and how he acquired it that might seem judgmental. In truth, I'm quite interested in what my son eats and why. Nor do I mention that, in this moment, I'm remembering that when I was a child, my parents acquired a pair of ring-necked doves that I named Lancelot and Guinevere. My father built a wide, floor-to-ceiling cage for them in the basement. These beautiful, gentle creatures and their many offspring were so tame that they'd sit on my finger or nestle in the palm of my hand. I loved their soothing, near constant hootings.

"Yup," he answered. "I shot these yesterday evening at Pawnee."

Ian rents this particular mobile home because it's less than a mile from Pawnee State Recreational Area where he hunts and fishes.

Inside the house, I sat at the table and watched as Brandy chopped vegetables and Ian washed the dove breasts and divided them into two piles of fifteen. One pile he grilled; the other, he sautéed.

~~~~

I've refrained from eating the flesh of any member of the animal kingdom for so long that I rarely think about what led me to this dietary lifestyle and ethical choice or why, forty-some years later, I still don't eat flesh. Now, I'm rarely asked to explain my choice since vegetarianism has become so common that most people not only know the foundational principles but may be vegetarians or vegans themselves or at least have tried one of these diets. But in 1981 when I became a vegetarian, most people didn't understand why I would choose such a seemingly austere or counter-cultural lifestyle or what the benefits of such a diet can be. Now, most physicians understand that one can be well-nourished without eating meat. But in those early years, an internist told me that I couldn't be healthy on a vegetarian diet, even though the blood tests he ordered proved otherwise. An obstetrician even told me that I couldn't have a healthy baby if I didn't make up for the lack of meat in my diet by drinking milk and taking iron pills while pregnant and lactating. (I swallowed a few iron pills but ignored his advice about the milk; both of my babies were well-nourished.) Now, I never find myself in a restaurant that doesn't offer me something more to eat than a salad and à la carte vegetables. But during the first couple of decades of my vegetarianism, even if I ordered something that seemed safe, like a bowl of vegetable soup and a side of beans, I might discover that the vegetables had been cooked in beef or chicken stock and the beans with bacon. When I was invited to dine in someone's home, I so hated to ask the host to accommodate my dietary choice that I often never said anything. But then I had to be prepared to offer assurances ("No, really! Rice and glazed carrots are plenty for me") and eat a sandwich once I returned home. Even when I (or more likely, someone else) stated my preferences in advance, it didn't necessarily turn out well ("I'm really sorry that you went to all of that trouble, but I don't eat fish"). More than two decades into the new millennium, though, it's so much easier to be a vegetarian. Airlines, hospitals, school cafeterias, and chain restaurants all accommodate us.

The first vegetarian I ever knew was Pete, a counsellor, teacher, and administrator at Iowa Wesleyan College, my undergraduate alma mater, and with whom I lived during my final semester. Before meeting Pete, I saw vegetarianism as an exotic, mysterious lifestyle that could never be a viable option since I had no idea what such people ate. Pete, who had little interest in cooking, didn't exactly offer a wide range of options. Every day he ate the same thing: granola, milk, fruit, and nuts for breakfast; a slab of heavy, grainy bread slathered with peanut butter and honey and topped with sunflower seeds and raisins for lunch; and curried brown rice, lentils, and mozzarella cheese, accompanied by a lettuce-and-sprouts salad with blue cheese dressing for dinner. For a break from this almost-always dinner routine, he might fry up a Loveburger: a veggie burger made from a dry mix that he bought at the food co-op in Iowa City, an hour away. He snacked on fresh and dried fruits, popcorn, and nuts. When I was with Pete, I ate what he did except for lunch. Instead, I made a cheese sandwich and a simple tossed salad. While I lost weight on this diet and was sometimes uncomfortably bloated, it turned out that I didn't miss meat. But at that point, I wouldn't have identified myself as a vegetarian. Then, I would have just said that I wasn't eating meat because we "ate other foods" at Pete's house.

Not long after I'd moved in with Pete, I visited my family for the weekend. When I arrived, I was hungry, so I grabbed the hunk of leftover T-bone steak I found in the refrigerator and ate it cold. It was cooked medium-rare, salted and peppered. As I chewed, it occurred to me that this was the first flesh of a mammal, bird, or fish that I'd eaten in several weeks. The steak was delicious, but I realized as I chewed that I didn't need it. That was the last time I ate meat.

The transition between an omnivorous and a vegetarian diet was nearly effortless for me. When I was a child, there were some meats I loved: fried or barbecued chicken, catsupy meatloaf, steak, and heavily processed ones like fish sticks or chipped beef. But others—liver, pot roast, fatty pork chops, or gristly minute steak—I found disgusting. When I'd gone away to college, I relished the dormitory cafeteria fare since I could eat what I wanted and, usually, that wasn't meat. In fact, I often skipped the hot food line and went straight to the well-stocked salad bar. I ate lots of yogurt, which I'd never had before college, as well as brown bread, vegetables, and desserts. But I wasn't yet a vegetarian. When I officially became one in February of 1981, I didn't have to wean myself off the taste and texture of meat as have others I've known who've made that same shift and commitment. Nor did I struggle with the sense that, without a meat dish, something essential was missing, especially when there were so many other items for me to partake of at any given meal.

When I told my great-aunt Pertsie about my new lifestyle, she asked, "What do you eat?"

"Everything but the meat," I answered, which seemed straightforward.

But she was still puzzled. "What will you eat at Thanksgiving dinner?" she asked.

"Well, I guess I'll eat mashed potatoes, sweet potatoes, cranberries, corn salad, green bean casserole, relishes, rolls, pumpkin pie, and whipped cream. Everything but the turkey and gravy. If the stuffing is made with pan drippings, I won't eat that either."

This dear woman, who loved to serve a big meal featuring a ham decorated with pineapple rings, maraschino cherries, and whole cloves, was perplexed. "But what do you eat?" she pleaded.

Eventually, I figured it out. If you asked her what she was serving for dinner, she'd tell you about the pork roast, fried chicken, or even the Spam, with no mention of salads, potatoes, vegetables, fruits, bread, or dessert. The meat defined the meal. To her, a meal with a bunch of what she saw as "side dishes," a meal with no center, was no meal at all.

Becoming a vegetarian, and calling myself one, mostly involved thinking of myself as such and arriving at a philosophical position to explain my choice. Since Pete had stopped eating meat for two reasons, he helped me with the latter. First, he found it unhealthy to eat animals that had been fed antibiotics and synthetic growth hormones. Nor was animal fat good for your heart. Second, Pete—who had grown up on a farm and knew what was involved in poultry and livestock production—felt that the vibrations associated with the violence of killing animals and the fear that act invoked in the doomed creatures interfered with his meditation and evolution toward blissful unity consciousness. (Pete was the first meditator I'd ever known, a practice which I also adopted.) I agreed with him that eating meat wasn't healthy, and I was at least open to his "bad vibrations" theory.

Early in my vegetarianism, I acquired a used copy of Francis

Moore Lappé's 1971 *Diet for a Small Planet*, which is now acknowledged as the first book to set forth the human and environmental costs of wasteful meat production. In my copy, I underlined several passages in which Lappé criticized U.S. agricultural policy for "the large quantities of humanly edible protein being fed to animals, and their inefficient conversion [of it] into protein for human consumption," a practice which she argued was the leading cause of global food shortages. World hunger worried me. During the early 1980s, newspapers carried photographs of the skeletal people perishing in the Ugandan famine, and I vividly remembered photographs from the 1970s of Bangladeshi children whose bellies were hideously swollen from severe caloric and protein deficiencies. The methods of food production that Lappé critiqued also caused environmental destruction because feedlot owners dumped staggering amounts of animal waste into our water systems and farmers relied too heavily on pesticides and synthetic fertilizers "to push the limits of the soil's productive capacity" in order to grow enough grain to feed all of their livestock and poultry. Lappé contended that we'd have fewer starving people and healthier soil and water if more people ate a more plant-based diet. How, I wondered, could anyone who cared a whit about other people continue buying and consuming animals raised under such conditions?

Lappé's book was more than a manifesto: it was also a how-to guide for would-be vegetarians. In it, she set forth the now-outdated theory that in order to consume enough usable protein from plants, one had to intelligently pair plant foods (for instance, rice and brewer's yeast or wheat and soy or sesame seeds and milk) so that, together, their incomplete proteins would create the "perfect balance" of essential amino acids in meat and eggs. To that end, she provided recipes with complementary proteins: garbanzo cheese salad, cornmeal-soy waffles, nutty bean tacos, sesame rice fritter puffs, masala dosai (brown rice and yellow split peas), and so on. I found Lappé's recipes too difficult to reproduce myself, largely because they called for ingredients I'd never heard of (raw bulgur? wheat germ? soy grits? sesame butter?), much less knew where to buy in the two places I call home: Iowa, long the nation's number one state in pork production, and Nebraska, one of our nation's leading beef-producing states.

Since I was learning about vegetarianism from the 1971 edition of Lappe's book, early in my experiments with plant-based nutrition, I worried about and worked hard at balancing amino acids so I could consume complete proteins. But I would discover that, in 1981, in the tenth anniversary edition of *Diet for a Small Planet*, Lappé retracted her earlier position on complementarianism, explaining that "in combating the myth that meat is the only way to get high-quality protein, I reinforced another myth. I gave the impression that in order to get enough protein without meat, considerable care was needed in choosing foods. Actually, it is much easier than I thought." Lappe clarified that unless the vegetarian's diet was overly dependent on fruit, some tubers, such as sweet potatoes or cassava, or on junk food, and if that vegetarian consumed enough calories, they were "virtually certain of getting enough protein" from plants. In the second edition of her book, Lappé even removed several charts, including one, "Summary of Complementary Protein Relationships," that I had studied carefully when I got my used copy of the 1971 edition. Vegetarianism was easier and even healthier than I'd originally thought.

While Pete and Lappé's concerns didn't influence my own choice to adopt a vegetarian diet, theirs were the reasons I *remained* a vegetarian and introduced my children to that lifestyle and form of activism. Ironically, Ian's biological father owned and managed an upscale barbecued pork rib restaurant in Omaha. Because he and I parted ways before Ian was born, it was easy raising my son as a vegetarian since it was just the two of us. But when Ian entered school, I gave him a choice: lunches from home (sandwiches made of cheese, egg, peanut butter and jelly, or a weird favorite of his, peanut butter and mayonnaise; cookies, fruit, and the dill pickles he loved) or from the school cafeteria. He chose the latter, and he relished it all: pizza burgers, wiener winks, tuna melts, chicken nuggets, creamed turkey on biscuits. I was troubled that he was eating the flesh of pigs that had spent their entire lives in gestation crates too small to turn around in or chickens and turkeys that had never known the pleasure of spreading their wings, scratching dirt, or foraging for worms, slugs, and seeds. But he'd made his choice, and I kept my opinions to myself since I was sure that there was more negativity and violence, more "bad vibrations," involved in forcing a child to follow a diet that wasn't what he wanted, a diet that might make him feel like an oddball among his peers, than in allowing him to eat foods I didn't approve of.

When Ian was six and I was a graduate student at University of Nebraska–Lincoln, I married a man who was a young assistant professor there. When I cooked for our family, I made vegetarian meals. When my then-husband cooked, he served meat-centered meals. At that point, Ian's transition to omnivorism was complete. After we divorced, I bought and cooked meat for Ian, which made me rather uncomfortable, but I wanted to respect his choice. When he was a teenager, I still bought the meat, but he cooked it.

Meredith, Ian's half-sister, also became an omnivore. After her father and I divorced, she ate very different repasts at her two homes. A typical post-divorce family dinner at my house usually included separate but overlapping meals: a vegetarian main dish—pasta, soup, pizza, stir fry, or wraps—for Meredith and me and a piece of meat for Ian, a salad or vegetable, and occasionally a dessert for the three of us to share. At her father's house, though, Meredith ate more meat-centered meals. She now says that the most memorable foods made by her father, a black man who grew up in Guyana, were his seafood and oxtail stews, chow mein, curried goat and chicken, barbecued ribs, pepper pot, "red" (corned beef), and the sweet potatoes or yams that he added to his soups and stews.

A vegetarian version of some of the foods that I enjoyed at my ex-husband's table are now part of my repertoire. For instance, his sister, who lived with us while she was a college student, would sometimes cook a big pot of white rice, black-eyed peas, onions, tomatoes, and a little stew meat in coconut milk, seasoned with more black pepper than most humans can handle. "Cook-up rice," she called it. I loved these flavors so much that I scooped out just the flavorful rice on top and ignored the fact that it had been cooked in the same pot as the meat. "It's best not to be too rigid about anything," I told myself. But after the divorce, I cooked a meatless version of "cook-up rice" for my children and me. Even though it was never as good as that which my former sister-in-law made, it was always a hit at potlucks.

Because of these distinct dietary influences, Meredith is a versatile and adventurous eater, who is sometimes an omnivore, sometimes a vegetarian, and sometimes a vegan. She will try any ethnic cuisine and has never turned down whatever wild creature Ian might be serving up. That said, she wasn't at my birthday dinner at which he served doves. By then, she'd moved to New York City for graduate school. But I remember an Easter dinner from a few years earlier when she and I entered Ian's home to find him cleaning carp—lots and lots of carp. He explained to his half-sister that Asian carp is a big problem in our part of the country since the invasive creature destroys the habitat of native fish, outcompeting them for nutrients and space. But there is a tasty solution to the problem: pulling carp from our rivers and lakes and then serving them in our homes and restaurants. "Carp is such an underrated fish in this country," Ian opined. Meredith, who had never eaten carp, found it good—bony, but good. I'm sure that she would have sampled his doves, too.

~~~~~

I don't remember what birthday gifts Ian and Brandy gave me when they served those doves for dinner, but I can still see the meal in detail. In the center of the table was a bowl of hot water in which we immersed rice wrappers just long enough to soften them. A pair of ceramic platters were loaded with mounds of shredded carrots, lettuce, and daikon radish; chopped tomatoes, green onions, and cucumbers; alfalfa sprouts; slices of seasoned, baked tofu; and then the mourning dove breasts, which reminded me of chicken gizzards. There were several kinds of sauces, but because the labels on some of the bottles were written in a language that I couldn't understand, I didn't know if they contained anchovies or shellfish. The safest option for me was the sweet-and-sour sauce. The wraps that Ian and Brandy rolled were tight, tidy affairs, with the dove meat as the main event and just enough vegetables and condiments to give them texture and color. I packed my spring roll wrappers so full of veggies and tofu that they fell apart. I had to eat them with a fork. And we all ate the bowls of Ian's spicy, sinus-draining squash soup.

No matter how surprised I am by an item on Ian's menu, I'm not surprised to find that he's still eating wild, still spending as much time outside as he can, since it's there that he feels most at home and at peace. When Ian was in his late teens and struggling to stay in school and out of trouble, he started hunting and fishing. Time spent in nature healed and guided him. He took its wildness into his body through the flesh of mourning doves, rabbits, racoons, wild turkeys, deer, pheasants, quail, turtles, bull frogs, crayfish, rabbits, walleye, and crappie. Their flesh and spirits nourished his own. Now, whether Ian is ice fishing in Minnesota or South Dakota, hunting mule deer in Western Nebraska, or stopping by Pawnee Lake to fish a bit on his way home from work, I'm comforted to know that he's doing what he loves and feeding himself with what he needs and craves. I like to believe that my intentionality about what and how I eat served as his model. I've never felt compelled to try to change Ian's mind so that his dietary beliefs might align with mine; that would have been a denial of who he is.

But not everyone in my family is as open-minded about the critters that Ian kills and eats. One Thanksgiving when my mother was visiting, she was worried about the type of meat he might bring to our holiday feast. Traditionally, Ian brings the meat; Brandy, a rich dessert; and Meredith and I prepare everything else. I told my mother that he'd probably contribute a wild turkey—not so different than what she herself would have bought at the grocery store for such a feast. But when Ian arrived with deer meat, horror flashed across her face. My mother had always been excited to see lovely, gentle deer browsing in her backyard, rotating their ears, lifting their tales, stomping their hooves. During deer hunting season, she would curse every time she heard a gun in the woods. Seeing fawns made her day. I reminded her that Ian was an ethical hunter. Unlike the plastic-wrapped cow or turkey meat on a Styrofoam tray that he could have bought and prepared for our meal—creatures raised under deplorable conditions, creatures killed and butchered by workers whose jobs are dangerous and underpaid—this deer had lived a wild, free life and had had a fair chance of escaping Ian's arrow or bullet. My mother seemed skeptical. But because Ian had provided the meat, she ate it—and even raved about it.

As an ardent proponent of ethical, conscious eating, I believe that people should not only be aware of where their food comes from and who was involved in producing it, but that whatever they eat becomes part of them—in more than just a nutritional sense. I believe that people should be intentional about only consuming foods that align with their moral principles. Ethical eating isn't just a diet but an attitude. A vegetarian who isn't educated about the ways in which food is, as Lappé says, "our most direct link with the nurturing earth," or who isn't aware of the ways in which their food choices affect others isn't an ethical eater. But an omnivore who is educated and aware that their food came from both the soil and living creatures might be an ethical eater. When I speak about the value of ethical eating, I'm more likely to talk about my son's version of it than mine since the principals of ethical meat eating are less familiar to most people than those of ethical vegetarianism and veganism. My son takes what he needs, doesn't waste any of it (what he doesn't eat of a deer, rabbit, or pheasant, he feeds to Duke and to Brandy's two little dogs), and doesn't ask anyone else to kill and clean the flesh that he consumes. He knows the true cost of what he eats. I respect that. Likewise, I only take what I need, don't waste any of it, and opt for organic over nonorganic foods since this mode of production is more respectful of the environment and those who produce the food I eat than industrial agricultural. And so I, too, know the true cost of what I eat, which is why I don't ask any member of the Kingdom Animalia to die for me.

While my son and I have different ideas about how to eat so that we cause the least harm to the self, to other people, to the environment, and to the creaturely world, we agree that the ideas we hold about what and how we eat express essential aspects of our identity. How we eat represents the moral codes we aspire to live by.

~~~~~

When we finished eating the spring rolls and soup at my birthday dinner, we were so full that we had to wait awhile before we could slice into the delectable carrot cake. We threw the table scraps to the chickens and roosters in the landlord's barnyard and returned to Ian's shady porch. My birthday, September 4, is just a few days into dove season, which runs until October 30. But Ian was already done dove hunting for that year. Since it's small and maneuvers easily and unpredictably on swift wings, *Zenaida macroura* is challenging game to pursue—and you have to kill quite a few doves to make a meal. (In Nebraska, the aggregate daily limit for this very abundant bird is fifteen. The possession limit is forty-five.) And yet a more pressing reason was this: that archery deer season had also opened on September 1. That following Saturday, Ian planned to be sitting in a deer stand in a blaze orange vest with his bow and arrow, the first step in refilling his deep freeze with deer meat. Some years, he easily achieves this goal. But in others, he has to supplement his wild meat stash with industrial meat from the grocery store. It's best not to be too rigid about anything.

As we chatted, we watched Duke try to herd the landlord's black cattle that were busy turning grass into hamburgers. We paused from our conversation to watch the occasional pickup truck fly past, raising dust on the gravel road. When Duke returned from his work, the half-dozen mourning doves that had been picking grit in the driveway rose on whirring wings and landed on the utility wire. I remembered that rain crows supposedly predict the rain, though I wasn't sure how since it seems to me that they're always cooing in response to any type of weather. I remembered how it felt to hold Lancelot's and Guinivere's warm, soft bodies in the palm of my hand. As the doves on the utility wire uttered their sweet, wistful call, I shut my eyes and listened: *oo-oo, oo, oo, oo.*

The Renoir

When I was seven or eight, my parents bought a framed print of Pierre-Auguste Renoir's "Oarsmen at Chatou" at an antique shop in Nauvoo, Illinois. If I was with them, I don't remember it. But I can imagine the circumstances. As the proprietor was wrapping the milk glass globes that my parents bought to cover the light bulbs on the chandelier in our living room, my mother saw "the Renoir," as she called it, hanging on the wall in a heavy, ornate gold frame, a real standout among the paintings of dreamy cottages in the woods or sublime landscapes by artists no one knows any more. I suppose that for my young parents, whose paychecks barely lasted until the end of the month, the extravagance of the thirty-five-mile pleasure drive down the Mississippi to the Nauvoo antique shop where they bought not what they needed but what they wanted made their purchases more precious to them.

For forty-some years, the Renoir hung over the television set in each of the five houses in which my parents lived. The only one where the extravagant, gilded frame fit its surroundings was the California bungalow with beamed ceilings, a fireplace with an enormous mirror hanging above the mantle, leaded windowpanes on either side, and bottom stairs that flared out and around the newel post. Where the painting and frame seemed most at odds with their surroundings was the prefabricated ranch-style house with an abundance of faux wood paneling, set on a horse acreage in rural Iowa where my parents moved after I left home.

When I was a child, there were several things that I loved about the Renoir. One was the presence in our home of a painting by a famous French artist set in an extravagant frame, which in my mind, made us richer and more cultured than our neighbors with their framed photographs of graduating seniors or John F. Kennedy or fussy floral arrangements, or bland bowls of fruit. Second, I loved the luminous dreaminess that Renoir had created with dabbed paint, broken brushstrokes, and a bright palette. But above all, I loved the grouping in the lower left quadrant of the painting.

Standing nearest the water and with his back to the viewer is a tall, dapper man in a straw hat, a white jacket, a black bow tie, and black trousers. He leans back slightly, his hands in his pockets, his left foot forward. His pose suggests self-assurance, maybe even arrogance. To his left, a man in a straw hat and dark clothing straddles the stern of the gig, his right hand resting on his cocked hip while he awaits the order to launch the boat. A third man, this one in a straw hat, a white shirt, and a black bow tie, sits in a two-person, orange-red rowboat with his back to the viewer. His face, dark dabs for eyes, mouth, and nose, is turned toward the three people on the shore behind him. His right hand holds the oar; his left hand beckons towards the empty seat across from him.

When I was a child, I saw the woman standing behind the dapper man as the focal point of the scene. She wears a blue, ankle-length skirt; a snug-fitting orange-red jacket, trimmed in frothy white lace; and a blue hat, with clump of orange-red flowers pinned to the side, the long ties knotted in a bow beneath her chin. What I so adored about this woman is that she hikes her skirt with her right hand, revealing her lacy, white petticoat. Will she climb into the boat, sit on the blue cushion, and allow the oarsman to row her across the water or will she remain on the shore with the haughty man who seems to be speaking for her?

SECOND IMPRESSION

During my twenties and thirties, years when I was earning college degrees, establishing myself as a high school teacher, then as a university instructor, and later as a professor, and finally getting my essays and books published, I had to know how things worked and why. Then, I was uneasy in the presence of vague ideas, ambiguity, ballpark estimates, something less than the right word, or a let's-wait-and-see attitude. I wanted the exact word, the full name, the clearest explanation, the most recent theory. In art, I wanted solid, realistic forms and clear, hard lines. Then, I wasn't content to say that the boat in Renoir's painting was orange-red; rather, I said that it was the color of a pomegranate to distinguish it from all the other orange-red possibilities. Likewise, I couldn't simply say that the woman wore a blue skirt. Rather, with the aid of a color chart, I determined that her skirt was a blend of blues: to be exact, Persian, a bright medium blue, and cornflower, a light lavender blue.

Then I was impatient with the Impressionists. Instead of offering sharp, resolute, and convincing details of scenes and objects, they offered soft, vaguely conveyed forms and general impressions of a sensory experience. What I was drawn to were the Flemish realism of Pieter Brueghel and the American realism of Andrew Wyeth and Edward Hopper. Then when I looked at the Renoir, it wasn't the scintillating colors that drew me, but the biographical facts behind the unfolding drama on the Left Bank and the context in which this painting was created.

I discovered that the model for the oarsman who gestures to the empty seat was Renoir's brother Edmond, a Parisian journalist. Gustave Caillebotte, a painter friend of Renoir and a rowboat enthusiast, is the model for one of the two men standing on the shore, though I don't know which. The woman flashing her petticoat is the vivacious Aline Charigot, who Renoir met the same year that he painted "Oarsmen at Chatou" and who soon became his favorite model and muse. Initially, Charigot, twenty years Renoir's junior, rejected her employer's marriage proposals because he refused to live in her hometown of Essoyes, some thirty miles northeast of Paris. Moreover, he didn't want children. But time and circumstances changed him. In 1890 when their son Pierre was five, Charigot and Renoir married. In 1895 they bought a house in Essoyes. When Aline died in 1915 and Pierre-Auguste four years later, they were buried there. Eventually, their three sons and a grandchild were buried there, too.

Intriguingly, the woman in the painting that is modeled upon Charigot gazes downward, away from her cocky companion and the gesturing oarsman and is on the verge of lifting her eyes to me or to whomever might be approaching from beyond the frame. Perhaps it is for this unseen presence that she lifts a corner of her skirt. I wonder, as I always do with painted or photographic portraits, if this is how the artist posed her or if she spontaneously turned from her companions to glance at the one with the searing brown eyes who was mixing pools of silky color at his easel and he, charmed by her sidelong look at him, rendered it on canvas. After she climbs into the boat, will she turn in her seat so that she is facing Chatou or will she keep her eyes on the receding shore, where the artist who stole her attention becomes smaller and smaller with each dip of the boatman's oar?

Chatou is a long, narrow island in the Seine where, in Renoir's day, affluent Parisians went to play. Many of the island's permanent residents tended the rental boats or cooked, cleaned, and served in the inns and cafés that provided refreshments and lodging for boating parties. In the Renoir, a barge the color of a pomegranate is parked near the shore. Beyond that is a stately, two-story white house with a pomegranate red roof and cornflower blue shutters. Farther in the distance are hazy green and white blotches—trees, people, houses, I suppose. No cormorants feed in the shallow waters of Renoir's Siene; no plump gulls screech on the dock.

As a child, I never thought about the distant shore. But in my twenties and thirties, I wanted to twist the focus ring until the blurred, indistinct contours clarified and sharpened like the almost photographic lines of Jean-Francois Millet's peasants or Gustave Courbet's nudes and landscapes. Then, I wanted enough detail that I could name the species of trees and read the lettering on the sign at the inn.

But certainty is not the point of Renoir's Impressionist works. In 1869 when he was twenty-eight, he and Claude Monet, sitting side by side, each painted the same views of La Grenouillere, a resort near the Seine frequented by working-class people. In my favorite of the series, Renoir painted the "camembert." A walkway connects the round, wooden dance floor floating on the water with the floating café. On this rocking wooden island are gathered a handful of bright but indistinct people standing in the water. The water shimmers with lavender, white, and shades of apple, lime, pear, and grass green. The trees are chartreuse and light-filled.

Renoir's and Monet's paintings of Le Grenouillere, considered the first Impressionist landscapes, bear the characteristic traits of this genre or movement. The paintings were done not in a studio from preliminary sketches or from memory but out of doors, in direct contact with the scene, in open air. Unlike the detailed, unembellished representations of the Realists, the Impressionists captured their subjective, momentary impressions and the changing light in a quick, sketch-like fashion. "Painters of mere impressions," one critic observed. "Wallpaper in its embryonic state is more finished than that seascape [of Monet's]," another charged. The Impressionists abandoned the sharpness of outlines or contours, which contributed to the misty, etherealness of their scenes. They used the newly-developed synthetic pigments that provided brighter colors than those favored by those in the art academies, and they placed pure, unmixed colors in surprising or complementary combinations, such as Persian blue and pomegranate orange, and let the viewer do the mixing. Rather than painting on a conventional dark-colored background, the Impressionists painted on light-colored canvases; they depicted shadows not with black or gray but with complementary or harmonizing colors that suggested shadows. In contrast to the blended brush-strokes and the smooth, flat surfaces favored by the academies, the Impressionists created a rough and irregular surface. Sometimes Renoir even applied paint with a palette knife. While academic painters applied a thick golden varnish to tone down and flatten the surface, the Impressionists wouldn't permit anything to dull their colors.

The subjects of the Impressionist paintings were also something new. Most academic paintings of the time focused on historical, mythological, or allegorical subjects—the birth of Venus, the coronation of a king, Samson subduing the Lion. The Impressionists, however, insisted that their paintings didn't have to have a subject. "What seems to me the most important thing about our movement is that we have freed painting from the subject," Renoir told his son Jean. "I can paint flowers and simply call them 'flowers' without their having a story."

Because of these revolutionary techniques and philosophies, the Impressionists were barred from exhibiting at the annual, government-sponsored, juried art show at the Academy of Fine Arts. In protest, they arranged their own exhibition, which they called the Exhibition of Rejects. In the 1870s and 1880s, Impressionism was the dominant artistic movement in France. Even though the Impressionists' exhibitions were met with mixed or critical reviews, Renoir was well paid for his work.

In 1879 when he was thirty-eight, a bright, pomegranate red and Persian blue period in his life, Renoir painted "Oarsmen at Chatou." Then he was deeply committed to the techniques and philosophies of the Impressionists. A few years later, he traveled to Italy, where he studied Raphael, Titian, and other painters of the Italian Renaissance. What he learned there moved him toward a "new classicism," in which he focused on line and form, as had the classical painters. And he went into the studio to paint. In the paintings of the ample, nude flesh of bathing women that Renoir worked on from 1884 to 1887 (Aline was one of his models), he contained their roundness with firmer lines than he'd ever used before. "It is a very good thing not to want to go on repeating oneself," the Impressionist painter Camille Pissarro said of the change in her friend's method. "But he has concentrated all his effort on line." Pissarro felt that what was missing in Renoir's new approach was "meaning." In my twenties and thirties, I appreciated those firm boundaries. But now I'm struck that the paintings from Renoir's "dry period" lack the vitality, the essence, the joy of life that is so present in his Impressionist paintings.

I've read that there is no sadness in Renoir's paintings, even in those from his old age. The last fifteen or so years of his life, he suffered mightily from muscular rheumatism, a disease that left him so crippled that he walked with two canes and was eventually confined to a wheelchair. To paint, this prolific artist who left the world some six thousand paintings, either strapped a brush to his arm or asked Gabrielle Renard, Aline's young cousin who modeled for Renoir and cared for his and Aline's children, to place the brush in his misshapen fingers and help him to push it across the canvas. In old age, the images that he painted—his wife, their children, their nanny, the flowers in their garden, the landscapes near their home—were solid and more clearly outlined than those from his Impressionistic period, though not as hard and dry as those from the mid-1880s. And still, his loose brushstrokes quivered with a brightness that age and disability couldn't extinguish.

THIRD IMPRESSION

After my father died, my mother imagined the day when she would live some place smaller and simpler and eventually, when she, too, would be gone. She wanted me to have the Renoir. She said that the faded print wasn't worth anything, though the frame was. But of course, I could never sell anything of hers. I imagined the thick, heavy gold frame hanging above my television, overwhelming everything else in my living room, reminding me of my parents, their houses, their day trip to Nauvoo, their absence. A wall all to itself is what this ornate frame deserves. But when I imagined the Renoir in a frame that is spare and black, yes, I could see it hanging in my living room (though not above the television), a seemingly moving mass of light and color contained by straight, black lines, at once the focal point and the complement to everything else in the room. Sometimes I regret not taking the painting, since my mother loved it so. But if I get lonely for it, I can visit my brother and sister-in-law and see it face-to-face, hanging in their house.

Now I can't say with certainty that the blues in Renoir's painting are Persian and cornflower since I see them differently when I view a reproduction in natural or electrical lighting. In fact, a slight change in the lighting or a slight shift in circumstances has challenged many of my certainties. Aging and decades of prayer and meditation have expanded my concept of time, space, and self, eroding the divisions between now and then, here and there, me and not me. Knowing people, including myself (especially myself), who despite our very best intentions have acted selfishly or ignobly, has made my ethics and standards less absolute, more flexible and forgiving. Changing tastes and innovations in the contemporary essay have so blurred the boundaries between, say, an essay where the actual and the imagined meet and a fictional story; an analytical, personal essay and conventional scholarship; an essay remarkable for its imaginative and linguistic leaps and a lyric poem, that I no longer can provide a definition of the form that is complete enough to include all the possibilities. Now it is not the finely detailed peasant scenes or landscapes of the Flemish School or the gritty urban scenes of the American Realists that I want hanging on the walls in my home and office, but the abstract art of Helen Frankenthaler, Jules Olitski, and Julie Mehretu with their insistence on visual impression over representation. What led me there is Renoir's vision that indefinite forms and general impressions can be a more faithful representation of experience and perception than that offered by the Realists.

When looking at the Renoir while on the far shore of middle age, I care far less about the provenance of the painting or my own memories of it or how I've seen it in the past than I do of my in-the-moment experience of the colors, textures, and light. As I gaze upon the painting, I imagine spending the afternoon watching the artist standing before an easel in the tall, olive and pear-green grasses near the Seine as light flows from his paintbrush. He reaches for the same tin paint tubes and mixes the same colors on his palette—orange-red, a few blues, yellow-green—as if there were no others. He paints the land, the water, and the people gathered around the pomegranate-colored boat not as solid forms but as patches of shimmering, vibrating light and color that demolish the idea of matter as substantial and impenetrable, as surely as do the quantum theories of modern physics.

The morning passes and I grow weary of watching the artist at work, so when the oarsman gestures toward the empty seat, I climb into the rocking boat and settle into the Persian blue–cushioned seat. It feels good to be gently rocking atop the water. The young man straddling the stern gives us a push. As the oarsman and I move across the water, I watch the forms on the Left Bank lose their edges. I turn and face the not-so-solid, distant bank of Chatou. Once there, I'll stroll away from the river and wander through the dabs and feathery strokes, the mere suggestions of faces and foliage. After my walk, I'll meet my friends for a late lunch in a sun-dappled café with a river view. As we talk, I'll watch the boats bobbing on the water and the small red and blue forms moving on the distant shore. Just before sundown, the oarsman and I will return to the boat.

As we move across the river, I care less and less about either shore. What absorbs my attention is the buoyant, tinkling words and laughter wafting across the glittering water and the shoosh of the oar plying it. I lean back in the seat and turn my face toward the shower of light created by short, fast brushstrokes of chalky blue, white, and a blush of pomegranate red, and the low sky, formed by rough and rapid brushstrokes of the same three colors. The sail on a distant boat carries a blue flame, at once shadow and light. It's not enough to move across the flickering surface while my limp fingers dangle in the cool water: I want to enter the luminescent river; I want to take it into myself.

The oarsman dips his single oar on one side and then the other, just as the artist on shore dips his brush in the white and the chalky-blue paint. Beads of sweat form on their foreheads and a tinge of pomegranate rises in their cheeks. I don't care if I ever reach land. Here in the open air, on the radiant water, under a blue, pomegranate, and white sky is where I want to be.

Common Magic

I'm sitting in a Pret de Manger in east London trying to catch up on the assignments from a couple of independent studies I'm directing. But I'm distracted. To my right sit three construction workers in chartreuse vests. They're probably working in the gutted building next to the coffee shop. I might find them attractive in a hunky sort of way if they were talking about something other than video games. To my left on the other side of an empty table sit two men. They strike me as an odd couple. The older man has buzzed blond hair, blue eyes, and crow's feet that suggest he's at least thirty-five. He wears a dark, fitted suit jacket, a white button up shirt open at the neck, and jeans. The younger man, probably twenty or so, with dark, tousled hair and glasses with heavy black frames, wears jeans and a charcoal and white T-shirt. He's literally sitting on the edge of his seat as he listens to the older man. Because I hear the word "job," and because the older man studies a sheet of paper that the younger man has handed him, I surmise that this is a job interview. The younger man seems earnest. No, he seems earnest and gullible. It's just a hunch I have, but the job that the older man is hiring for may be a little shady, like selling door-to-door what nobody wants—electric brooms, boxes of greeting cards, crates of grapefruits, or magazine subscriptions.

I try to settle into my work. But the younger man is tossing coins from hand to hand. He opens his right hand with a flourish, and they're gone! He opens that hand again and there they are. Just as the older man begins to speak, one of the construction workers shouts, "Yeh, man!" and they all laugh. I wish they'd leave so I could hear what the odd couple is saying. I recognize the eager look on the younger man's face, since I've seen it on the faces of some of my students. I probably looked that way, too, long ago in the presence of a published writer who was willing to teach me what I hadn't been able to figure out on my own about crafting essays. The younger man is the hungry novitiate, the magician in training. The older man is his mentor.

Each man spreads a rectangular piece of dark-blue velvet cloth on the table and sets out big bottle caps. The teacher appears to be giving directions to his student, but with the talking and laughing at the table to my right, I can't hear what he's saying.

I Google "magic" on my laptop. The Wikipedia entry on "Magic (illusion)" lists the effects that illusionists perform: productions, penetrations, transformations, restorations, transpositions, transportations. That such extraordinary acts as changing a red scarf into a blue one or a smashed watch into a whole and workable one would bear such everyday names as "transformation" or "restoration" is rather disorienting. When I search what one must do to become a magician, I learn that since magicians don't like to reveal their tricks, most aspirants join a magic club or pick up the art on their own. I Google "magic lessons." Over 5,460,000 hits. Apparently, someone *is* sharing secrets.

I've never liked magic acts. I'm bothered by the deceitfulness of concealment, and I'd feel foolish if a magician pulled a silver dollar from my nose. Yet I'm grateful for real magic—like wishing for coins to plug a parking meter when I have no change and then finding a quarter right there on the ground near the meter, which gives me enough time to run into a shop and get change. But is that luck or coincidence rather than magic? Real magic is when, with the aid of supernatural forces, you cause something outside of yourself to conform to your will. Turning pennies turn into quarters. Or traveling from Nebraska to London and back with the click of my heels rather than in a stuffy, smelly, germy, crowded, over-priced, airborne aluminum tube. But that type of magic is beyond the scope of my powers.

I've experienced "magical" moments. "Magical" as in captivating, charming, enchanting. Among my most precious memories are these: an August evening when I was eleven and stood with my family in reverent silence on a pier jutting into Lake Michigan, gazing at the lights from a distant city and their twinkling reflections on the water, while lulled by the sound of the waves; a jaunt on a Mississippi cruise boat when my mother and I stood together on the upper deck, the wind in our faces, savoring the moment together on the river on whose banks we'd both grown up near but now both lived so far from and in opposite directions from each other; watching uncommon redhead ducks as well as everyday waterfowl drift on the water at a state park with my son on Thanksgiving morning, my first true outing following surgery to replace the hip that a bicyclist had broken when he ran over me. What makes these moments magical is the sense of oneness or communion that obliterates the distinctions I usually insist upon between inside and outside, between me and not me.

"Time, mates!" one of the construction workers calls as he checks his phone. My wish has come true. The mates drain their cups, clean up their food wrappers, and vanish. Now I can hear the magician and magician-in-training. But they're picking up their bottle caps and folding up their velvet cloths. Perhaps one of them also said, "Time, mate."

"Oh," the mentor says, as if he just remembered. "Let me see your jacket."

The student pulls from his backpack a wrinkled orange linen jacket. It's not the lurid orange of a plastic drug store jack-o-lantern but the subdued orange of a real pumpkin. The young man stands up and slips it on. It looks odd with his tee shirt and messy hair. Because of the cut and that it's short, as jackets go, I wonder if he found this in the women's department. If it were my size, I'd wear it with a slim, silky scarf. What would better complement that orange—a turquoise or a bright green?

The jacket is boxy and doesn't nicely hug the younger man's shoulders. But the lapels are slim, which is good given his slight frame, and the venting in the back will allow him to move freely as he saws a woman in half. He twitches his shoulders and tugs at the front flaps.

"The jacket is bad," the older man says flatly.

The younger man's shoulders sag. He drops into his seat.

I'm taken aback by the mentor's bluntness. Aren't the Brits supposed to be more polite and reserved than we Yanks? I want to argue with the mentor. His student is low on funds, especially now that he's paying for private magic lessons, and this jacket from the bargain rack at TK Maxx is all that he can afford. He chose this pumpkin orange jacket over the tan one because he thought it would be a real attention-getter at children's birthday parties or when he sets up a table on a corner near the farmer's market and does card tricks for tips. The student wanted a frank assessment of his jacket choice, but this seemed insensitive. I'm tender with my students and always tell them what I appreciate about their writing before telling them what they need to work on. If I were the magic teacher, I would have said to my protégé, "What a fetching color you've chosen. I like it. But . . ."

"It's the sleeves," the mentor says.

The sleeves? They end at the hinge of wrist bone as they should—or at least, that's the way most people like them. They're fine.

"The fabric is too stiff," the teacher says. "You want stretchability in case you have to pull a bouquet or a dove out of your sleeve." The mentor smiles. His judgment about the jacket is based not on color or style, but on fit and functionality.

The student looks surprised, as if he'd never considered this.

The two men pick up their cups and walk toward the door. I can't collect my items fast enough to follow them and hear what they're saying. By the time I exit the shop, they've vanished.

Over lunch I tell my daughter a story about two magicians and a pumpkin-orange jacket. She likes the turn in the story about my misjudgment as to why the teacher didn't like his student's jacket. "I wish that you could have seen him in that jacket," I say. We both agree that most of the time, it's better to withhold judgment, especially when we're out of our element.

As we're walking toward the Tube station on a street that's so crowded, I'm afraid that my daughter and I will be separated in this city of 8.8 million people where I barely know anyone and don't know my way around. I keep my eyes on her. But then, something calls me to look at the crowd and I see a familiar face there, a face that touches me. It's the magician-in-training hurrying past, his backpack slung over a shoulder. "That's him!" I say to my daughter. "It's the guy in my story! Can you believe it?" But before I can call out to him and tell him that I sat near him in the coffee shop, that I like his jacket, that I wish him well with his career, he disappears into the crowd.

After Dover

The trek up the steep, shoulderless road from Dover Castle to the top of Langdon Cliff was dicey. At some points, the road was so twisty that we couldn't see oncoming traffic until it was upon us, and the cars approached from what I saw as the wrong direction. When Meredith and I heard one draw near, we stepped off the narrow road into the weeds until it passed. I considered that the journey might not be worth the risk and that we should head back to where we came from. But if we turned around now, we wouldn't experience the white cliffs of Dover. Surely I'd be haunted by the lost opportunity. And, too, I suspected that this travail-filled hike, should we complete it, would contribute atmosphere and tension to whatever story I'd tell about my journey to that iconic landscape on my first trip to England. So we pushed on.

At the crest of the hill, a dazzling blue, white, and green world opened before us: the Strait of Dover, the narrowest part of the English Channel. I felt unbounded and triumphant. On the grassy cliff top, several people walked dogs. A gray-haired man and woman sitting on lawn chairs, blankets covering their legs on this cool, windy July day and books face down in their laps, gazed over the water. A group of hikers with backpacks strode by on the trail. I could see part of the cliff face to our north: white limestone streaked with black flint. But I had to take it on faith that the cliff on which we stood also had a magnificent face, since it was too dangerous for us to step over the fence, stand near the crumbly brink, and peer down. From this vantage point, I could look across the channel to France and imagine what I'd see if I approached this beach and these cliffs from the east—taller than Big Ben, taller than the ancient Buddhas of Bamiyan that the Taliban destroyed, taller than the Statue of Liberty.

During our tour of Dover Castle that morning, we'd learned of the legions who had landed or had attempted to land at the foot of the cliff on which we stood: Julius Caesar and the Romans in the mid-first century BC; the Vikings during their ninth-, tenth-, and eleventh-century raids of Kent; William the Conqueror and the Normans in the eleventh century; Napoleon and La Grande Armée in the early nineteenth century; the Germans during World War II. In the twelfth century, Henry II built Dover Castle so that this fortress on high would be the first thing anyone saw when crossing the channel from the east. Now, some anticipated another invasion. Across the twenty-three-mile channel at an encampment in Calais, some three thousand people fleeing war, corrupt regimes, and the effects of global climate disruption in Syria, Pakistan, Eritrea, Sudan, Afghanistan, and other countries were seeking to enter England or to remain in France. What possibilities might they have imagined when they looked across the channel at the white cliff upon which my daughter and I stood? Though I pay scant attention to the news when traveling, I had heard that some of the migrants living in the camp were so desperate or foolish or courageous that they undertook perilous means of reaching British soil.

We sat on the only bench that wasn't occupied and savored the scene. The intense blueness of the sky paled nearer the water; the darker blueness of the water grew greener nearer the land. (Are there enough names to capture these gradations of blue, green, and blue green?) Distant boats appeared to be stationary. Grasses waved and bent in the wind. I pointed to the path that led over the cliff to our north. "Wanna follow it?" I asked. "Not yet," Meredith said. For now she was content just to observe. Once I settled in, I realized that I was, too. In fact, there was no place I'd rather be than sitting in comfortable silence next to my daughter before this bright expanse. No longer was I curious about where the trail led. When thoughts arose—the risky trek back to the castle and on to the bus depot; my desire to know the names of the blue butterfly and the yellow flowers at my feet; my fear that Meredith would settle in Europe, even farther from our Nebraska home than New York City, where she then lived; my fear that my mother's worsening abdominal pain was caused by something more serious than reflux—I let go of them. I mused about the story that I might one day tell about this radiant, wonderstruck moment that we shared and my deep gratitude for the privilege and good fortune that had brought us here. Then, I let go of that, too.

Eventually my attention settled on the harbor below, the site of the world's busiest passenger ferry port. I've never found a commercial hub fascinating, much less beautiful or engrossing, but this one was. How precisely managed, how finely orchestrated was the flow of this heavy traffic! Slow queues of lorries rolled onto massive ferries to be conveyed across the channel to Calais or Dunkirk; other semitrucks deboarded the vessels and drove onto a multi-lane roadway. Freighters, cruise ships, border patrol boats, and sailboats drifted in and out of the harbor through the breakwater or waited in the jetties. On land were rows of parked lorries; the many buildings were unremarkable except for the bold turquoise one. A tiny lighthouse topped each end of the breakwater. Above it all, seagulls glided, and wispy clouds drifted. Across the water, a white cap floated upon the land: Calais. I imagined Eurostar, a sleek, high-speed train blazing through a tube beneath the channel, 244 feet below sea level at the deepest point. Meredith had suggested that we take this train to Paris. But I'd rather single-handedly row a boat carrying the two of us and our luggage across the choppy waters of the channel than be enclosed in a thirty-one-mile tunnel beneath the weight of all that dark water.

Since we'd spent most of the day touring the castle, we had but a few hours on the cliff top before we had to hike down the hill and catch our bus back to Canterbury where we were staying. As a memento of our day, I pocketed a small piece of chalk, so soft and powdery that I wondered how these cliffs had stood as long as they had against the erosive work of time and water. Before making our descent, we stopped in the Gateway to the White Cliffs of Dover Visitor Centre for water and restrooms. I had the crazy hope that someone there might offer us a ride, though of course, neither of us would ever get into a stranger's car. How many things could go wrong in that situation? I asked the receptionist, a polite, proper man in his sixties, if there was a bus that would take us down the hill—even though I knew there wasn't—in hopes that he knew of another option. No bus, he said, as he led us to a map on the wall. There, he showed us a footpath that offered a more direct and safer route into Dover than the one we'd taken from the castle. From there, it was but a short walk to the bus station. Meredith photographed the map. Then we chatted with the receptionist about his interest in Americana (especially Woody Guthrie and Gillian Welch) and our Airbnb over a fragrant, sometimes noisy Chinese restaurant in Canterbury, the city where he and his husband lived.

As we headed east, away from the visitor's center and toward the path to Dover, a car pulled up and idled beside us. I felt a flash of panic. "I'm driving to Canterbury. Do you want a ride?" the driver asked. It was the Americana-loving receptionist. Meredith and I looked at each other. Do we? At that moment, a woman in her sixties approached. She and the man in the car greeted each other by name and chatted for a few minutes through his open car window. "I've known him for fourteen years," the woman said to us. "He's a good guy. You'll be safe with him." What doubly good fortune! Certainly, this would be part of the story I'd weave about our day at Dover: the fortuitous offer of assistance; the immediate assurance of safety from what seemed to be a trustworthy source. And so, we climbed into our new acquaintance's little car. As we sped down the M20, our knight in shining armor told us about the historic preservation that he and his husband had undertaken on their home, which was centuries older than the United States, and we laughed a lot as we discussed the differences between American and British television series. What a fine ending this good luck and these moments of cross-cultural connection would provide for my essay.

In a few days, Meredith and I crossed the channel, not by Eurostar but by Air France. We explored Paris for five days and London for two more before I returned to Nebraska, and she boarded a train for Berlin where she met up with her next travel companion. In London, we stayed with my ex-husband's aunt and uncle, who'd lived in the same narrow row house in East Ham since they immigrated to England from Guyana in the 1950s. Because of her training as a nurse and his as an electrician and because they were both native English speakers, they'd been sought after immigrants by a country desperate for workers. Yet, this lovely couple grumbled about the foreigners from Pakistan and Bangladesh who'd so drastically changed the character of their neighborhood.

Once back home, I went to work crafting a straightforward, reflective essay about the silent, keenly aware state that my daughter and I had shared on the park bench above Dover Beach and our serendipitous encounter with a stranger. But my essay was too simple and not entirely honest, since there were details I'd omitted. Some I could easily weave into my story. For instance, I could include a sentence or two in the opening paragraph about my cranky outburst about the nature of our hike to the cliff top. Owning up to my regrettable behavior could enhance the story by making the persona I'd created more relatable and trustworthy.

But there was another loose end that was harder to ravel. Not long after I returned home, I discovered that a mere twelve or thirteen hours after Meredith and I gazed across the channel at ethereal Calais, a migrant would die of the injuries he sustained while trying to jump onto a train that was traveling, via the bottom of the channel, from Calais to England. Despite my efforts, I couldn't find his name, age, or place of origin in any of the news reports I checked, much less what interested me more: the circumstances that he was fleeing from in his home country; how he'd made his way to France; what he hoped to find in England. Did he, for instance, imagine himself emerging from his underwater train ride unscathed and triumphant, born into a new life in England that included safe shelter, enough food, steady, paid labor, and the resources to support a family—or at least the dream of a family?

While I found nothing about the migrant, I found plenty about the effects of his death on channel traffic. After his body was discovered at 5:30 on the morning of July 7, 2015, authorities enacted Operation Stack in which they slowed or halted traffic headed for the tunnels by ordering lorries to park on the M20 and by diverting non-freight traffic from that superhighway. Freight Transport Association Chief Executive David Wells said that disruptions, such as that caused by the migrant's death at the French port, were costing the freight companies "hundreds of millions of pounds each week." This faceless, nameless man whose death had halted tunnel traffic until 7:00 on the evening of July 7 was one of at least fifteen migrants who would die in such a brutal manner in the months to come. Because the effect of these deaths on the traffic flow, in October of 2016 French authorities would demolish the "Calais Jungle," the temporary home of as many as eight thousand refugees and migrants who were awaiting the opportunity to enter England or for their applications for asylum in France to be approved.

Many of us have had to revise a memory after learning of new, relevant information, say, the context for a remark that we'd dismissed as insignificant or had taken offense at. Such discoveries can so alter our view of our past that thereafter, we divide our related memories into those that occurred before and those that occurred after the consequential event. If only we could fold up these vexing revelations, pack them in a box, and send them back where they came from, far, far away from us.

I couldn't leave the story of the man who died in the tunnel out of my essay. In part, my interest in him and the other migrants and refugees was humanitarian. Just what was one to do when civil war, religious extremism, natural disaster, or deep poverty made violence, persecution, chaos, and dire want everyday occurrences in one's homeplace? In part, I was moved to fold him into my story because of the coincidence of the migrant and me being in the same place at the same time. While my circumstances—that I was deep into my fifties before I had the liberty and the resources to travel internationally to some of the places I'd long dreamed of—were so different from those of the migrant's, I could well imagine his yearning to reach British soil. But perhaps the most compelling reason for including the story of this seemingly peripheral figure in my essay is that I'm intrigued by the extent to which the addition of one new detail can change the story we tell about ourselves and our experiences, reminding us that the first version we tell about any encounter might not be the truest.

Even so, I regret that I was able to relish my memory of a magical afternoon at Dover Beach on July 6, 2015, for but a few days before the migrant asserted himself into it, disrupting the contours, texture, mood, and meaning. I regret that I couldn't keep from wondering what became of his body, what his loved ones must have endured as they waited for news from or about him, how they dealt with that ambiguous loss, or if, on a different day, on a different train, he might have made it to England, perhaps finding shelter, work, place of worship, and community, perhaps even in East Ham. But what makes me uneasy is this: I don't regret the unexpected twist, complexity, and balancing ballast that he brings to what otherwise would have been a pleasant, uncomplicated narrative. Even before I mentioned him directly, his wordless presence was there, rustling in the underbrush and casting a long shadow over what, for a brief while, was a bright, serene, and splendid afternoon spent with my daughter at the White Cliffs of Dover on my first trip to England.

Leaving the Body

A woman enters the room and sits a basin of water on the bedside table. "I'm here to get your mother ready for the people who are coming to pick her up soon," she says softly. My brothers and sister-in-law excuse themselves and head to the family lounge. I linger.

"Can I stay?" I ask.

"Of course," the woman says. She wears a pink uniform and has long, straight dark hair. Perhaps she's a nurse's aide, since she wasn't one of the women who brought morphine in response to my repeated runs to the nurse's station in the several hours before my mother's heart stopped beating. She dips a cloth in the water and wrings it out. I wonder the point of bathing my mother, since her body will soon be ash.

"I just want you to know," the aide says, "I always talk to the person I'm washing. I don't want you to be alarmed." Then she turns to my mother, whose heart stopped beating less than an hour ago. "I'm going to give you a bath, Patricia. I'm going to start with your face."

I find this comforting, this informing my mother of what's about to be done to her, since I can feel that something of her is still here.

The aide wipes my mother's forehead and cheeks, her eyes, the corners of her mouth. "Now I'm going to wash your hands and arms, Patricia," she says, as she works the washcloth over each arthritic finger on my mother's left hand.

When I was a child, my mother believed it would make me sicker if I took a full bath or got my hair wet when I was feverish.

Instead, she'd wipe me with a warm washcloth. A "sponge bath" she called it. It wasn't as good as a real bath, but I liked the attention. I wish that I or someone else had thought to do this for her before her heart stopped beating.

When I look up, I see that another aide, this one in a light turquoise uniform, has entered the room. She watches as the aide in pink removes the IV needle taped to my mother's right forearm. My mother hasn't received anything through this needle since she entered the hospice facility three and a half days earlier. I wonder why it wasn't removed until now.

"I'm going to take off your gown, Patricia," she says. She unties the johnny gown, and the two women slip it off. The pink aide carefully pulls the catheter.

It has been so long since I've seen my mother's naked body, and I'm filled with wonder. Even though she would feel shamed by my scrutiny, I want to savor and memorize the details. Her nipples are a lovely light pink and pegged; a puckery white surgical scar on her left outer breast is smaller than I expect it to be and matches one that I have on my right breast. A dark pink surgical scar follows the lower edge of her right rib cage; her belly is swollen as if she were pregnant and the skin taut and yellowish. Her vulva is bald but for sparse reddish hairs. Her once stout legs are thin, the skin loose and wrinkled. I know their shape so well: large knee bones, slightly bowing calves, like those of her mother, and thick ankles. Just below her right knee on her inner calf is a blue vein, an inch or two long, that has been there as long as I can remember.

Her feet are puffy and mottled. The little toe on her right foot is flattened atop her fourth toe. Something was wrong with that toe or foot when she was a baby, though I can't remember what; nor can I ask her about it now. The doctor taped it wrong, and the toe bone insisted on holding that position after the tape was removed. Before buying a pair of sandals, my mother had to test the placement of the straps in relation to her "bad" toe. Though the fourth toe on my right foot looks normal, it is also bad, perhaps broken without my knowing it and never healed right. To accommodate my bad toe, I buy my walking shoes a half size larger than my other shoes. As I gaze upon my mother's scarred and shriveled body, I wonder if this is how I'll look in another twenty-one years.

I used to be almost as familiar with my mother's body as my own. When she was pregnant with her youngest child, an August baby, she'd walk around our unairconditioned house in just her underwear, her belly hard and enormous and scored by red stretch marks. I was old enough to be embarrassed by her near nudity.

I remember her sunbathing in the backyard in a two-piece swimsuit. If she was on her stomach, I could see the light freckling that appeared when she tanned or burned, the big flesh-colored mole just above her bra strap, her slender waist, the silvery-white stretch marks on her wide, fleshy hips. If she was on her back, I could see her breasts fallen to the sides (they were so much larger than mine ever would be, even when swollen with milk), the blue vein beneath her knee, her thick ankles, and her bad toe. Until I left home, we used to brush each other's hair and give each other "back scratchin's." "Get it really good around my mole," she'd say.

Aging turned my mother's body into something that was foreign and yet familiar in a way that unsettled me. When I visited her three months prior to her death, I glimpsed her in her bedroom, pulling on her jeans. Because I didn't want to embarrass her by letting her know that I'd seen the slack, wizened, and folded flesh on her buttocks and thighs, I quickly dropped my gaze. But she had seen. "It's okay," she said. "You can come in."

Then, she asked if I wanted to see her incision, cut so a surgeon could lift from her body her tumor- and stone-filled gallbladder and the excruciating pain it had caused her the past few months. But he left behind the cancer that had spread throughout her peritoneum. "No point in removing it," he said. "This cancer is too aggressive." My mother laid on her bed and pulled up her sweater. I placed my hands just below the cut on her soft belly and prayed for healing. I prayed so long and so deeply that, finally, she interrupted me. "Are you all right?"

Now, less than an hour after my mother's heart stopped beating and a little more than an hour before the couple from the funeral home will arrive, I find myself starving for her physicality.

"I want to touch her," I say to the pink aide. I don't want to alarm her by doing so without first announcing my intention.

"Of course," she says. "Go ahead."

If I were alone with my mother, I would run my hands up and down her arms, kiss each palm, taste each palm, touch the scars on both knees, try to rub warmth into each cold foot, and press my hands flat in the hollow between her breasts where her heart once beat. Instead, I lay my hands on her hard, warm belly and the big "tumor load," as the hospice doctor called it. I kiss her clean forehead and stroke the top of her head.

What is it that I'll be missing now that my mother's heart has stopped beating, and she'll soon be turned to ash? For most of my adult life, she and I have been separated by demanding schedules, too many miles, and costly plane tickets. Until this past year when I visited her several times, we usually saw each other twice a year, with me staying with her for a week or so in the summer at her log home in the woods of north-central Ohio and her staying with me at my home in Lincoln, Nebraska for several days in the fall or at Thanksgiving or Christmas when my son and daughter were also there.

Yet I always imagined that one day she and I would live near enough that we could meet regularly for lunch or a concert or a play, shopping in thrift stores or at farmer's markets, and visiting each other in our homes. What I regret the most is that we didn't spend more time in each other's physical presence. This sponge bath is my last chance to see and touch and smell my mother, flesh of my flesh, my first home.

Since my father's death almost ten years ago, I was present to my mother almost every morning when we'd talk by telephone for half an hour, though often longer, while I walked in my neighborhood or on the bike path. If one of us wasn't available then, I'd call in the late afternoon or early evening.

We'd talk about the weather ("Tell me about your weather, because whatever you got is coming our way."), politics ("I just wish that Hillary was more electable, because I'd sure like to see her and Bill back in the White House."), British series on PBS with *Call the Midwife, Doc Martin*, and *Foyle's War* being our mutual favorites ("They must have an awfully small pool of actors over there in England, because you keep seeing the same ones in different series."), her longtime beau ("Can't live with him, can't live without him," she'd often say), aging ("Sometimes I look in the mirror and go to pieces."), my kids ("What's going on in Meredith's world?" "Is it safe to ask how Ian's doing?"), her friends ("Mary Jane and I had so much fun getting lost yesterday!"), her memories ("Grandma Whitaker said I was born with a caul over my face. She said she wore it in a locket around her neck for good luck, though I never saw it."), and the afterlife ("Is it wrong to want there to be nothing after death?").

But we rarely talked about her cancer. What I wanted to know was what it was like to watch and feel one's body shutting down as one's end approached. What I wanted to know about were her regrets and gratitudes, her doubts and certainties, and all those details she held about my life and hers that I never knew or only knew pieces of or had forgotten—details that no one else can tell me. Instead, we talked about the little facts of her illness: her sleep, appetite, nausea, and defecation. The daily "S.A.N.D." report, I called it. I was frustrated, but my mother said that if she wasn't thinking or talking directly about the big facts of her illness, she could forget about it and feel "normal" for a bit.

For the most part, what has been taken from me, now that my mother's heart has stopped beating and her body will soon be turned to ash, isn't her body, since over the past several decades that was so seldom part of my experience of her, but her disembodied voice, words, thoughts, laughter, and silences transmitted across 850 miles by radio waves.

Several times a day over the next several months after my mother's heart stopped beating, I'll feel the urge to call or text her and tell her about this weirdly warm February and highly allergenic March, the unexpected death of a Supreme Court judge, the article in our hometown newspaper about the volunteer work of one of her former teaching colleagues, the sad and daunting task of sorting through her possessions ("If I only have room for one more item on the truck, should I take your sewing rocker or the corner what-not shelf that Dad built?"), and how less urgent and consuming my prayers are now that she's gone. I'll want to tell her that I feel gut-sick when I see how quickly her name is moving down the list of frequently called numbers on my cell phone.

I'll want to tell her that I now hold so many poignant memories that will forever define my experience of the seasons. For instance, when returning from several of my daily rambles last August and September, I stopped in a neighbor's yard to pick ripe pears with one hand while holding my cell phone in the other as my mother and I talked about her pain level at that moment, about what the surgeon might find, did find, and how Dad lived with cancer almost ten years instead of the three that the oncologist predicted. Or fall, her favorite season. The ten days we spent together in mid-October were so beautiful, in part because our faith in the chemotherapy was newly borne and fervent. Or early winter. During my visit the first week of January, I watched her precipitous decline; later that month, I witnessed the swift approach of her savage death.

Every morning after my mother's heart stopped beating, I'll think about all that I would ask her if only she'd answer her phone—like what should I do with the pears? The first time I saw the clear bags of sliced pears stacked in my freezer after her heart stopped beating, I cried. Now, I can't eat them; nor can I throw them out. I'll want to assure her that in spite of the pain, I don't want this grief that mingles with my joy at the arrival of the mourning doves and daffodils she loved, and I don't want the buds on the pear trees to end because it keeps her near and present.

The two aides turn my mother onto her belly and wash her back. I see the big mole, the slack, silvery stretch marks on the sides of her torso, the brown splotch on her bony butt—the beginning of a bedsore, the turquoise aide says. "Already?" I ask.

My mother's cancer spread with what the hospice doctor called "reckless abandon." "If I had to have a cancer," he said, "this isn't the one I'd pick."

She had gone from living alone in her own home to two nights in the hospital and three and a half days in hospice before her heart stopped beating. When I'd visited her two and a half weeks earlier, she'd been thin, weak, and exhausted, but we'd shopped, gone to church, consulted with an attorney about her financial affairs, exchanged sharp words over what she later called "a tempest in a teapot," and met her boyfriend for lunch (she'd eaten shrimp and coconut cream pie, two of her favorites, and laughed as he teased her).

One of the first things she said to me when I arrived at her bedside in hospice after the red eye flights that I'd purchased that same day for my son and me was, "I'd thought I'd have more time." The second thing she said was, "I'm so sorry to put you through this."

I had thought that she'd die the following fall, as her oncologist had predicted, rather than in January. So certain was I that we would "have more time," that for the spring and fall semesters, I shifted my classes at the university from the traditional face-to-face format to a hybrid or blended one, alternating equally between classroom and online meetings. I figured that this more flexible combination would allow me to spend generous stretches of time with my mother at her home and eventually, to care for her in my home when her end was near.

Soon I'd regret having moved half of my class meetings out of the classroom and interacting with my students as disembodied posts on Blackboard. There we can't make eye contact, read each other's facial expressions and body language in light of the context, as consoling or unnerving as that can be, hear each other's laughter, participate in a communal silence, or notice a new haircut or tattoo. Even so, the dean of my college is awarding bonuses to faculty who redesign their courses so that there's more screen time and less or no in-person time.

And too, I'd regret that so many of my interactions with friends, both near and far, are done via Facebook, as if a photograph, a brief comment, or a "like" from my hundreds of cyber friends, many of whom I've never met in person, could ever fill my heart. I miss seeing children playing outside in my neighborhood and am sad and worried that instead of learning how to get along with and enjoy real people, they're in their homes, sitting alone before lit screens, true and unquestioning believers in the illusion of connectivity they're offered there.

Even though I can access almost all the public library holdings online, I pop in at my branch library at least once a week. As I browse through the books and DVDs, I chat with the librarians, security guards, and volunteers shelving books, watch preschoolers flip through books or play with blocks and puzzles, and try to ignore the intrusions made by people and their phones. On a recent library trip, I saw two little boys slouched in armchairs near the children's section, surrounded by bright and enticing book, magazine, and audio-visual displays. Each held a ticket reserving a computer; each looked bored and dejected. "We'll have fun as soon as we can get on a computer, right?" one said to the other.

The women finish washing my mother. They tuck a clean sheet around all but her face. The transformation is almost complete.

The day before my mother's heart stopped beating, I asked her if she wanted me to comb her hair. "God, yes," she said in a lucid moment. But she was in such pain that I was afraid to move her. I combed what was free but left the snarled mess beneath her head. I dig in my mother's purse until I find her comb and two hair bands. While the pink aide holds my mother's head up, I scoop the tangled hair out from beneath. "I'm going to comb this out, Mom, and give you the best, most even, tightest braid you've ever had. I'll be gentle." I ask the turquoise aide if I can have a pair of scissors and a big envelope. Carefully, I work the comb through the knots.

When I was growing up, my mother wore her thick, curly red hair short with a little height on top, feathery bangs, and shorter, face-framing hairs. But when she was in her late fifties, she stopped cutting it in the back. Her mullet, we called it. She'd email photos to me of her braid so that I could see how long it was getting. When I was in Paris during the last summer of her life, I found a barrette at the gift shop at the Musee Marmottan Monet bearing a tawny and soft blue detail from a Monet painting of two women carrying parasols. Mom loved the Impressionists, and she loved pretty things for her hair, so I bought it and sent it to her. When I was at her house later on the day that her heart stopped beating and was filling her suitcase with mementos to take home with me, I found the barrette not in the bathroom drawer crammed full of her other hair accessories but in a dainty, black-and-white cloth drawstring bag on the vanity. I put it in the suitcase.

Mom had been relieved when her doctor told her that she wouldn't go bald from chemotherapy. But she said that her hair had grown thinner because of what she preferred to call "my treatment." Twice, I clean hairs from the comb and throw them away. As I comb, I splay her long red-gray hair on the pillow. "It's so pretty, Mom." I regret that I never told her this before, though I often commented on how long her hair was and how remarkable it was that it was still reddish, even at seventy, even at eighty.

I pull her hairs together, divide them into three parts, and plait, tightly, evenly, and bind the braid at both ends with the bands: this, the final raveling. I position the scissors just above the top band, close to her head. The scissors gulp and chew. This feels like a desecration until I remember that her hair will be the first part of her to become ash when she is cremated. Though her hair is thin, I'm surprised at how many bites of it I must take with the scissors. Suddenly, the braid and a triangular chunk of hair from the left side of her head are light and free in my hand. This rope of my mother's DNA is my relic, memento, remnant, heirloom. I slide the braid into the envelope and tuck what's left of her hair behind her head.

I will frame the braid and hang it . . . where? In my living room for all to see? In a part of my house where only I go? I will pick a frame that opens easily, so I can touch and smell the braid whenever I need to. Or will I just keep it in the envelope? I hope that she is pleased that I want more than just memories of her body.

My mother is clean, shorn, and tucked in, her body out of sight. The aides leave the room. I am sad that our work is done. I kiss her forehead.

I fetch my brothers and sister-in-law. Once we're back in the room, we eat the snacks that the chaplain brought us the day before and tell stories about our childhoods that make us laugh, as we wait for the couple from the funeral home to load and strap my mother's corpse onto a gurney and take it away.

Fleet

Throughout my elementary school years, my brother and I spent part of our Christmas vacations at our grandparents' house. More than just forty-five miles separated them from us. Their house—a house that someone else owned—had no basement and was heated by a stove. They lived next to Elder's store which had a penny candy counter, often ate on tray tables while watching TV, paid a neighbor, Alice, to clean their house on Wednesdays, and sometimes let me sleep in the front room on a chaise lounge lawn chair padded with blankets. Beneath a frantic cuckoo clock, an air conditioner jutted from their front window. No one I knew had either of those.

Each New Year's Eve, Jamie and I prepared a celebration for the four of us. We draped our homemade paper chains around the front room. We made piles of confetti by cutting construction paper into tiny pieces—a tedious job. For our holiday supper, we ate frozen pizza that Granny cut into wedges with her kitchen shears and slices of my favorite dessert: Newly Weds ice cream wedding cake roll. We pretended that our root beer was real beer. When we deemed it late enough (we never made it to midnight), Jamie and I hollered, "Happy New Year!" as we jumped and threw confetti. For a spectacular moment, the bright pieces landed upon our upturned faces and outstretched hands. To prolong our moment of delight, we'd scoop handfuls of confetti from the floor and throw them at each other. Paps, sitting in his easy chair, feigned offense as he waited for us to brush the confetti from his hair, arms, and lap. Someone swept up the pieces of our hard work, though I don't remember who.

When I was eleven, I was mopey about what I didn't know then would be the last New Year's Eve I'd spend with my grandparents. It seemed babyish to hang paper chains and toss confetti in their shabby, rented house when what I really wanted was to go to a slumber party at a friend's house. "Oh, Archie," Granny said to Paps. "Missy's already outgrowed us."

~~~~

The busy intersection of North Twenty-seventh Street and Cornhusker Highway is a dispiriting place. On the northwest corner is a no-frills grocery where I occasionally shop. In the adjacent strip mall is a liquor store, a nail salon, the Nebraska wic program office, and a really awful Chinese restaurant. On the southwest corner is a temp employment agency ("Jobs! ¡Trabajos!") and a seedy motel where many of the vehicles in the parking lot are old and battered. Sometimes I see people dashing across the highway toward the motel, carrying bags from the grocery and liquor stores. South of this intersection on North Twenty-seventh and within blocks of each other are three charities. Between them, you can get a hot meal, a shower, and after school tutoring. This is an opportune place to be down and out or to volunteer your time helping the down and out. Several years ago, I helped serve meals and read books to the kids at one of those charities. On the northeast corner of this intersection where there's now a tanning salon and a Home Depot beyond, there had been a bait shop, where my son, my then boyfriend, and I bought nightcrawlers for our fishing trip at Branched Oak Lake. Then, all this land now covered by asphalt and brick and mortar was planted in corn or soybeans.

I'm at this intersection often, since my comfortable, mostly paid for house is a about a mile away. My plan was to live there for three years; I'd find and settle into my ideal home and my realer life in some place other than Nebraska. But twelve years later, I'm still in the in-between, still making do. If something reminds me how swiftly these years have passed, years I thought I'd spend differently and elsewhere, I'm uneasy, because I know that whether I remain in my provisional life and home or finally find and claim the one that I imagined and yearned for, the years ahead will slip by even faster. How easily a day becomes a decade.

While I'm waiting for the light to change, something breaks into tiny pieces. They fall before me like confetti. Golden confetti. I don't know if they're coming from within or beyond me. Or perhaps they're coming from the God who sometimes speaks by filling the sky with stars and whirlwinds, manna and angels, rain like stones, and chariots and pillars of fire. When I see the sunlit, golden pieces drifting down, I have the good sense to stop fiddling with the radio, to stop contemplating where I've been and where I'm going, to stop thinking and to just watch. The sparkling pieces don't land on cars and pavement; nor are they taken by the wind. They fall, and then they're gone. The light turns green.

A place so lacking in beauty, a place where I never expected to pass so much of my life, a place where I'm always alone because that is how I now move through most of my days, strikes me as an unworthy setting for this dazzling vision. And yet, what better place for beauty and blessedness to fall so unexpectedly and to vanish just as quickly than here?

Free Samples

I pull into the U-Stop Convenience Shop, the last place to buy gas on North Twenty-seventh before you cross or merge onto Interstate 80. I sort of know what I'm looking for. The four photographs I've seen of him reveal that he's tall, wears wire-rimmed glasses, and has short light hair. Yet none of the photos offer a clear, close shot of his face. Just minutes earlier on the telephone, he told me that he drives a white Malibu with customized license plates bearing the shortened version of his last name, which I recognize as his username on the internet match-making site where we "met." It's what everyone calls him, he says. I wonder if I'll call him that, too, someday.

Twenty minutes together is all we have. He drove into the city this morning for shopping. He wanted to meet me for lunch, but I had a brunch to attend in the late morning and a memorial service in the afternoon. A brief interview for a date is what this is. Within twenty minutes, we will determine if we merit a full weekend evening of each other's time. From my experiences with other men I've met on the match-making website, I can usually determine that within twenty seconds and usually, my answer is either "probably not" or "absolutely not." In recent years, each of the men that I've kept company with for more than a few dates were ones that I met the old-fashioned and rather random way—while giving a reading at a coffee house; while waiting too long for service at the Verizon store; while washing clothes at a laundromat during that brief window of time between the breakdown of my old washer and my purchase of a new one; while rallying at the state capitol in opposition to the TransCanada pipeline.

What I'm looking for. I sort of know what that is at this point in life: deep friendship and a little romance. What I don't know is if I'm willing, yet again, to invest the time and energy and openness that it takes to really get to know and feel comfortable enough with a man that we can treasure, worry over, and receive solace and joy from each other, or if I'm out of love.

A man sits on a bench outside the double doors of the U-Stop Convenience Shop, his long legs stretched out in front of him. I recognize the glasses but the hair that I saw in his photos is gone. "Candidate for a Date" or "C. D." rises from the bench and watches me pull in next to his Malibu. He is smiling. I wave him over to my car and point to the passenger seat. I shove the seat in my little Honda Civic as far back as it will go. As C. D. eases himself into the seat and folds each long leg into a high, sharp angle, he tells me that it's better for us to sit in my car than on the bench because the wind was messing with the hair on his shaved head. The joke could have been amusing, but it goes on too long. Then he explains it. But of course, it really doesn't matter what we are saying because what we're after is a good look at each other's faces—the eyes and the mouth, especially the eyes. His face is pleasant, and his eyes are blue and attentive.

We chat about real estate. He tells me about the century-old farmhouse that he bought, lifted, and moved several miles to the little Nebraska town where he's lived the past couple of decades. He refurbished every inch of it, doing all the work himself, including removing the asbestos-filled slate siding and replacing it with vinyl. I tell him I moved far north so I'd be closer to the interstate and so, closer to my job in Omaha. Yet years later, I still don't feel at home in this part of Lincoln. I long to return to one of the old, friendly, walkable neighborhoods nearer the geographical center of the city. But I can't sell my house without paying at least $12,000 to cover the realtor's fee and then there's the difference between what I owe on the house and what it's now worth. Before I can sell my house, I have to paint or side it, but because the house was built in the late '60s, back when they still used lead paint . . .

C. D. puts his hand on my arm and I stop talking. I suppose that I was going on and on and now I'm mildly embarrassed. "There's a dog in traffic," he says. The cars and trucks in the two northbound lanes of North Twenty-seventh have stopped. "I bet he jumped out of the car when his owner stopped for gas or something." C. D. pauses. "Look! He's coming this way."

"I'll go get him," I say. I hop out of the car and run toward the stopped vehicles. Some dogs are so rattled around traffic. They run erratically, zigzagging like squirrels, confusing everyone. There . . . there it's coming toward me. It's tiny, with a tight, barrel-shaped body, and stumpy little legs. I don't like that type of dog with its fast, mincing, ridiculous-looking steps. I prefer the more confident, graceful stride of a taller, longer-legged dog. Even so, I don't want to see this little one with the bright black eyes spattered on the pavement or hear its piercing, dying yaps.

"Here, puppy," I say, as I bend down and extend a hand. It's so tiny and pure white, an older dog, an older dog with a collar. If it will let me, I'll scoop it up in my arms, take it back to the car, call animal control, and wait. In that impulsive moment, I don't consider the possible outcomes of this act: that it might take so long for someone from Animal Control to come for the dog that I'll miss the funeral of the old acquaintance, a woman who was younger than me and with a daughter still in high school; that no one comes for the dog *ever*, and I'm stuck with it; and the least likely scenario, that the dog moves my heart and I can't let it go, even though another dog is pretty much the last thing that I want or need. But when the dog sees me, it veers and heads toward the Cracker Barrel Old Country Store and Restaurant. I give up.

As I walk back to my car, I realize that I've just given C. D. quite a bit of information about me—that, depending on his interpretation, I'm the type of woman who has such compassion for a dog in harm's way that she attempts to rescue it or that I'm the type of woman who acts rashly, leaving a stranger in her car with her purse and keys; how I move when I run; how I look from behind, specifically my hair and my butt. Or maybe he had his eyes on the dog the whole time. If so, I want to know that.

"Gone," I say, as I slide into my seat. I pull my cell phone out of my purse and call Animal Control.

"Animal Control is one of your favorites?" he asks.

I nod. I realize that C. D. might think that I call Animal Control with frequency because I'm a real dog lover. But actually, I've listed that phone number as one of my "favorites" because on too many of my daily rambles in city parks and neighborhoods, I've been threatened by dogs at large. Once, I was even run down, attacked, and bitten by a boxer. The puncture wounds on my leg healed long before the nightmares about the attack faded. In truth, I am the type of woman that reports dangerous dogs and files complaints against their negligent owners, *and* I rescue dogs in traffic. When I get off the phone, I tell C. D. that apparently others have called about the dog, too, since the woman who answered asked me if the dog I was seeing was "a little white one with a collar." Someone from Animal Control will be here soon, I tell him. We wish the dog well.

C. D. says that he's sorry my job has been so stressful lately, something I shared with him in an email message earlier in the week. I'm touched that he remembers that. We talk about workplace politics and how much we both dislike meetings and those folks who won't let the meeting end until they've said everything they have to say at least three times. Then, we both see it at the same time a bird whose form is familiar to me but whose plumage is like nothing I've ever seen. "I think it's a blackbird," C. D. says.

"It's shaped like a blackbird but it's not black," I say. The feathers are light brown and highlighted with the oranges and pinks of a sunrise or of orange and raspberry sherbet. "It would be beautiful if it weren't so weird," I say. We watch the bird stride past the car toward the front doors of the U-Stop.

"Weird," he says, as he slowly nods. Then the bird flies away. Runaway dogs and bizarre yet beautiful birds. I feel like I'm watching a parable, with all its familiar yet strange, ordinary yet extraordinary imagery unfurling before me. If I can tease out the meaning beyond the immediate and the apparent, perhaps these parables will tell me something essential about this man or my own intentions.

I wonder if C. D. is the kind of guy that can see the parabolic potential in seemingly random everyday events. I'm about to ask him something along that line when he nonchalantly announces that he has bats in his attic. I'm not sure if he's being straight with me or if he's making another joke, with an explanation to follow. Or maybe he's easing into a parable.

"You know how you usually have flies in your house this time of year and you don't know where they came from?" He slowly shakes his head from side to side. "I don't have any, so you know there's something wrong.

"I took a lawn chair out in the yard the other evening and sat there and watched the attic. There they came. The bats. It can't be good to have bats in your attic. It's not hygienic," he says, scrunching up his nose.

"No, it's not," I agree. "They're up there defecating, urinating, shedding, and who knows what else." I don't say anything about rabies because I've heard that contrary to what most people think, the incidence of that disease in bats is no higher than that of any other wild mammal. Besides, I like bats. They use echolocation to locate and capture their prey; the females raise their young in nursery colonies of dozens or hundreds; and as a summer evening edges toward night, these flying folded shadows straight out of the Eocene Epoch dart and veer overhead and suddenly drop out of sight. I would never spread erroneous and potentially injurious information about bats. But neither do I want one anywhere near me, unless I've been forewarned of its presence.

"There are only two kinds of bats that these can be in Nebraska. Big Brown Bats or Little Brown Bats." C. D.'s "b's" are slightly bombastic. "A Little Brown Bat is about the size of a mouse when it's like this." He crosses his arms over his chest and hunches his back like a sleeping bat. His shoulders almost touch his knees. Then he sits up straight again. "They're only this big," he says as he spreads his thumb and second finger a few inches. His nails are clean and nicely clipped. "But the bats that I have are a lot bigger." He nods for emphasis. "They're Big Brown Bats.

"I got on the internet and found a humane way to evict them. You make a valve tube out of a two-inch diameter plastic pipe or caulk tube. You cut it so it's about six to eight inches long." He shows me these distances by spreading his thumb and second finger. "You take a piece of plastic netting—you don't want the mesh more than a sixth of an inch—and tape it to one side of the exterior opening on the pipe. Then you thread the tube through the opening in the roof where you saw the bats coming out. The bats can get out through the tube, but they say that because of the netting, they can't get back in. Well, I think they can't climb back in because their claws can't get a grip on the hard plastic surface in the tube. Once you see that there aren't any more bats coming out of your attic, you seal off the entry points." C. D. has been looking over the top of his glasses at North Twenty-seventh as he delivers this tutorial, but now, he turns and looks at me. His eyes are quite blue and sincere. "But I'm not evicting them just yet. It can still get pretty cold at night in April. I don't want them to suffer."

"That's a good plan," I say. "And you only have to wait a few more weeks until it's warm enough that you can give them the boot."

Like the other candidates that I met first in cyberspace and then face-to-face in restaurants, parks, coffee houses, and now, a convenience store parking lot, this man is gainfully employed, kind, politically progressive, not unattractive, and on cordial yet detached terms with his ex-wife, and so meets my minimum standards. There is nothing particularly wrong with him, though his imitation of the sleeping bat was a little weird. But neither is there anything particularly right about him, though I was touched by his remark about his unwillingness to make Big Brown Bats suffer from the cold. Because of that remark, I move him from the "definitely not," past the "probably not," and into the "perhaps we'll get together again" category.

I tell C. D. that I need to leave for the memorial service and that I have a big pile of student essays to grade this weekend. He tells me that he needs to get some chores done at home because on Sunday morning he's heading out for an epic bike ride from the small town where he lives all the way to a little speck of a town near the Nebraska-Kansas border.

At this moment, it's not Candidate for a Date in a nylon Lycra full body suit leaning into a turn that I'm imagining, but the produce aisle at the grocery store. I picture the free sample lady, the one with the big, coal-black hairdo, red lips, and big, jingly, often holiday-themed earrings, placing a corn chip on each of the napkins that she's laid out. Customers can take a chip and dip it in one of the three bowls of salsa, each filled with a different and new-fangled flavor, say, peach-mango, pineapple-jalapeno, or tequila. Nearby in a clear plastic globe are wedges of blood oranges that you serve yourself on a toothpick. On a typical Saturday morning, the walk past the meat counter is a bit of an obstacle course, because of the various stations where you can sample Little Smokies sausage, shaved hickory-smoked ham on a snack cracker, and if you wait just a minute, a tiny chunk of the beef hissing and popping in an electric frying pan. In the bakery, a woman fills tiny plastic pill cups with dabs of pineapple or blueberry cheesecake. "Go on," she says to me with a wink. "You can take one of each."

There's an etiquette that you should follow when sampling. You should feign interest in the product even if you don't like it or if all you really want is a bite of free food. If the free sample lady is passing out coupons, you should take one, look it over and ask a question or nod your head to show your approval. You can throw the coupon away later. And always thank her for giving you the opportunity to try something you'd never buy or something that you never knew you wanted until now.

At this moment in the parking lot outside the U-Stop Convenience Shop on North Twenty-seventh Street in Lincoln, Nebraska, what I wish for are free samples, tiny dollops of the quotidian scooped from a typical day ten years hence, served in plastic pill cups with tiny plastic spoons. In the first free sample, I see myself rising from my bed to close the window because the temperature falls so fast on an April night in Nebraska. Before I let the curtain fall back in place, I turn and see a single pillow positioned in the center of the head of my empty bed. But in the second sample, when I turn from the window, I see this man's sleeping face illuminated by a slat of moonlight and framed by the pillow on his side of the bed. In both scenarios, what I most want to see is the unguarded look on my face when I turn from the window and see my empty or occupied bed. Is it contentment? Wonder? Dismay? Desire? Contempt? Ambivalence? Gratitude? If I could see my expression, I would know what to do and say in this parting moment before I take my leave of this man who is considerate of bats.

Before he gets out of my car, C. D. and I shake hands. I thank him for the opportunity to meet. "We'll be in touch," he says. I nod. And if we aren't, I want him to know, it has far more to do with me than with him.

Giving Form to Feeling

Across from the entrance to the main gallery hangs a life-size painting of a naked, elderly woman. Visitors can't not see it. More shocking than the woman's loose, salmon-pink and yellow flesh is that she holds a black pistol in each hand. She aims one at the viewer—me—and the other at her left temple. I gasp. Until I wandered into this gallery at the Museum of Modern Art (MoMA) in PS 1 in search of an engaging way to pass several hours while my daughter taught violin lessons at a nearby academy, I'd never heard of Maria Lassnig, nor had I ever seen *Du, oder Ich? (You, or Me?)*, the 2005 self-portrait that she painted when she was eighty-five. As I stand before this confrontational image, I wonder if the artist is an exhibitionist or if something happened to her that she found so unbearable that she's willing to commit murder or die by suicide in response. Or is she bluffing, in which case, the joke is on me?

I take my leave of Lassnig and her weapons to explore the sixty-nine years' worth of paintings and films of hers on display in the lovely old school building in Long Island City, New York. At first I supposed that the painted faces I encounter—pained, shocked, perplexed, pathetic, monstrous, brooding, and occasionally placid (or is it stoic?)—are those of people she encountered in her waking or dreaming life. But according to an exhibition placard, her focus was on representing her "internal world." In fact, in most of the paintings that curator Peter Eleey and assistant curator Jacelyn Miller chose to display are self-portraits.

These aren't achieved by the artist painting what she sees in the mirror. Rather, these are depictions of her essence and of what she thinks and feels about the world. So, what I encounter are images of Lassnig merged with unlikely objects (a cheese grater, a muzzle, a piece of red meat about to be squeezed in a potato press) or animals (a bull, an elephant, a rabbit). It's the artist swathed in clear plastic wrap. It's the artist disguised (green skin and goggles) or deformed (two eyes, two noses, two mouths). It's the artist wearing an overturned saucepan on her head, blinded by the white mush covering her forehead and eyes, her mouth agape. It's the artist naked from the waist up, calmly steadying the pole piercing her chest. I am transfixed by these images, some baffling, some whimsical; some nightmarish; and I wouldn't hang any of them in my home.

As I work my way through the exhibition, I learn about Lassnig from museum placards and information that I pull up on my cell phone. At twenty-one, she enrolled at the Academy of Fine Arts in Vienna. The Nazis, who then controlled Austria, were so provincial and reactionary, prizing what Lassnig called realistic "pictures of peasants," that they forbade students to even read about Expressionism, the art movement that most intrigued her. Shortly after leaving the academy, she developed the philosophy of *Korpergefuhl* (body sensation or physical feeling) and *Korperbewusstein* (body awareness or consciousness). Body awareness, according to one placard, is Lassnig's approach to painting in which she depicted her physical sensations at the moment of painting, rather than picturing herself objectively as she might appear in mirrors or photographs, the latter being the more common approach to self-portraiture. Through this abstracted, self-referential approach, so at odds with what she was taught at the academy, Lassnig portrayed how she *felt*, thus closing the gap between sensation and articulation. "Not drawing a rear end because you know what it looks like but drawing the rear end feeling," she told Brigitte Werneburg in a 2010 interview.

In a 1980 journal entry, Lassnig described the process of depicting her awareness of her body as she was sitting:

> Resting on one arm, one feels the shoulder blade, of the arm itself only the upper part, the palms of the hands like the grips on a crutch . . . I feel the points where my backside presses into the divan, my stomach because it is filled like a sack, my head is sunken into the cardboard box of the shoulder blades, the skull is open at the back, in my face I feel the nasal opening, as big as a pig's, and around it I feel the skin burning. I'll paint it red.

Because Lassnig only painted what she felt, she left out those body parts that she wasn't aware of—often the top of her head or her feet. Nor did she paint her ears, since she lost her hearing, or her hair, since it lacked nerve endings. Because of her inward-looking focus, she felt that she didn't need the mood, atmosphere, or context that setting provided. So, most of her images hang in empty space.

Lassnig likened her efforts at giving form to feeling to "fencing in clouds." She briefly corralled them and then painted them fast—in three or four hours—as she might not have the same feeling later, according to Hans Werner Poschauko, a former student of hers and her assistant at the time of her death. The versions of herself that she painted based on such awarenesses are raw, distorted, monstrous, or bizarre, which makes me wonder if she ever felt whole, beautiful, and at peace. If Lassnig had poured her time and attention into painting landscapes or still lifes or realistic "pictures of peasants," would she have felt her fears, pains, and sorrows and her bodily sensations less keenly?

~~~~~~

When I return to the main gallery, I find Lassnig waiting for me. The hard, black gun barrel flush against her left temple is jarring compared to the soft pastels of her nude flesh. Knowing that at any moment she could end this standoff by pulling one or both triggers makes me squeamish. What could I say or do to placate her?

On our initial encounter, what stood out to me (other than those guns she's brandishing) were her sagging pink breasts, her pouchy, pink-yellow belly, her splayed, yellow-gold thighs, and her bald vulva. But on this second viewing, I notice that she has no ears or eyebrows and that the top of her head is gone (blown off?). Her left eye gazes straight ahead, but her right eye looks to the right. The auburn line tracing her forehead suggests hair. Her wild blue eyes with pinpoint pupils and pink gaping mouth suggest shock, horror, or fear. Her hands grip the pistols so tightly that they're red. Finally, I notice that her body is sloppily bordered from the top of her head to her waist with vibrant turquoise (a color I love), mild yellow where her left ear should be, and a dab of chartreuse. Her upper body appears bright, bold, and alive. Because she didn't outline her lower half, it seems as though it lacked the electrical emanations of her upper body, or that she wasn't as aware of it, or that she lost interest in the project before completing it. Her right leg is lopped off mid-calf and the other, just above the knee. Without feet, this woman isn't going anywhere. I wish for a setting to provide contextual clues. Is Lassnig in her bedroom? Studio? Subway? Nursing home? Café? City park? Wherever she is, surely she commandeered the situation.

In 1960 Lassnig left the male-dominated art world of Vienna for more education and artistic freedom in Paris. In her early years there, she produced line paintings like the chartreuse, blue, and yellow shapes and red-orange dots in *Figur mit Blauem Hals (Figure with a Blue Neck)* or the rather people-ish shapes (one short and stout, one tall and lean) in red and various blues in *Napoleon und Brigitte Bardot*. I revise my initial opinion that her work is too disturbing to hang in my house, since I'd love to have either of these bright images in my living or dining rooms.

In 1968 at the age of forty-nine, Lassnig left Paris for New York City, lured there by the freedoms and promises of feminism. "The country of strong women," she called the United States. What the art-viewing public wanted then wasn't her sometimes awkward, sometimes cartoonish, and often unsettling self-portraits, but Pop Art, performance art, minimalism, conceptualism, and photography. To pay the bills, she reviewed art exhibitions for Austrian newspapers and painted realistic, commissioned portraits and backgrounds for animated films. Americans "make you uncomplicated, whether you want to be or not," she told Werneburg. But it wasn't the seemingly straight-forwardness of Americans that Lassnig prized, but complexity.

She also valued artistic range. "I have been working long enough to establish my own tradition," she said, "from realism through surrealism, art informel, automatism, and I don't know how many other isms." Some of the "isms" that Lassnig explored but didn't include in this list are Impressionism, Expressionism, Tachism, Automatism, and Cubism. This diversity in subgenres explains why some of her works in the MoMA exhibition are so drastically different from each other that I wouldn't have recognized them as being created by the same person. Compare, for instance, her 1956 "Self-portrait/Abstract Head" comprised of a sloppy column of blocks in muted browns, oranges, greens, and blues with the lurid representation of *Du, oder Ich?*

In the 1970s Lassnig entered what she called her "American Realism period," which she described as "green light without colours." Apparently, this approach was simple enough that Americans could understand and so, appreciate it. In one of these paintings, *Self Portrait under Plastic* (1972), she presents a surprisingly conventional view of herself as a somber woman in possession of all her facial features, rare among her self-portraits: blue eyes with contracted pupils, high, rosy cheekbones, upturned nose, thin lips, downturned mouth, and shoulder-length brown hair against a bland green background. Draped around her face and neck is a sheet of clear plastic. Though she's not deformed, disfigured, hybridized, or missing essential parts, because of the restrictions that the veil imposes, this self-image is also disturbing. The woman appears silent and passive, unwilling or unable to remove the plastic from her face or to ask for help. Lassnig began painting herself sheathed in plastic after noticing that fruit and vegetables in American supermarkets were plastic wrapped, something she'd never seen before and that struck her as odd. Had she placed the plastic film around her head or had she felt as if had someone had done that to her? Was it cultural forces or the effects of trauma that so enshrouded her? Was the film there to keep her safe from contact with tainted or germy others? Or was it there to suffocate her? Perhaps this is how it felt to Lassnig to gain approval only when producing art that was blandly realistic, blandly colored, and blandly simple while those works of hers that she most cared about were ignored or scoffed at. Perhaps this is how it felt to watch Andy Warhol gain fame and money for churning out bland, unimaginative images of the industrial commercial economy—soup cans, Coke bottles, and reworkings of someone else's images of celebrities. Because of the plastic film, the artist and I can't see each other with clarity, but if she speaks, I might be able to make out her muffled words. Speak to me, Maria! I'm all ears.

Because people weren't buying those paintings of hers that mattered the most to her, Lassnig studied animation and filmmaking at the School of Visual Arts in New York City and made amusing, autobiographical, feminist animations. The MoMA exhibit included multiple showings of *Kantate*, a seven-minute film that Lassnig made in 1992. As she croons in German a sing-songy, fourteen-verse story of her life ("The Ballad of Maria Lassnig") against a drone-like accompaniment, she appears in various costumes—gangster, bride, cowgirl, Native American, punkster, court jester, Tarzan, femme fatale with a yellow boa, the Statue of Liberty. With her petite frame, chestnut hair, funky glasses, and bright, lively eyes, I find her perky, playful, and far prettier than the faces in any of her self-portraits. It's illuminating to hear her sing of the strife in her childhood home and of her mother's sadness, the bullying she received in a Catholic school, her commitment to art, the unappealing men she encountered in Austria, her departure and later return to her home country, her love of skiing, television, and motorcycling, and how she benefitted from devoting herself to art. But these various images of her and the cartoonish background in the film strike me as trifling compared to what I find in her paintings.

In 1980 Lassnig accepted the first professorship granted to a woman at the art academy in Vienna. There, she delved into the Expressionistic style for which she's best known. She also established Austria's first animation studio. Attention for her work in her natal country was long overdue. In fact, she didn't have her first major solo show in Austria until 1993 when she was seventy-three. By the time Lassnig received the international attention she craved and deserved, it was almost too late. One year before she died, the Venice Biennale, an international visual arts organization, conferred upon her the Golden Lions award for her life's work.

Lassnig addressed her decision not to marry or have children in two paintings displayed side by side at MoMA. In *Illusion of the Missed Marriages II* (1998), a naked, brown woman sitting in bed is bent beneath the weight of a man that she holds above her head like a barbell. She's aged; he's young. She's solid and fleshy; he's translucent and ghostly, though clothed. The woman is scalpless and missing part of her right ear; he nonchalantly smokes an after-sex cigarette. Clearly, Lassnig saw marriage as a heavy load to bear. Yet she seems to have struck a balance of sorts between the need for companionship and inspiration and the freedom to create by asking her lovers—artists, a jazz musician, a restauranteur, and others, many of whom were younger than her—to model for her, which allowed her to work while spending time with them.

Lassnig also saw motherhood as taking more than it gave. In

Illusion of the Missed Motherhood (1998), a naked, sickly green, orange, and yellow crouching creature grasps her knees as a lifeless form comprised of white bars emerges from her vagina. The woman is bald and earless; her almost human face is sad with puffy, red-pink cheeks. "When I was young, I was clever enough to know that if I got married or had children, I would be eaten, I would be sick if I couldn't paint, and I would be schizophrenic because I would have wanted to [both paint and raise a family]. So, I renounced it," she's quoted as saying in Randy Kennedy's obituary about her in the *New York Times*. But, too, one can view *Illusion of the Missed Motherhood* as making a statement about her relationship with art critics and viewers who saw her creations as stillborn or malformed, each a poorly executed caricature.

It's Lassnig's paintings from the 1980s and 1990s, in which she portrayed herself as having the attributes of machines or aliens or humans with prostheses, that make me the most anxious. These are the hardest ones to behold. In *Language Grid* (1999), which hangs to the left of *Du, oder Ich?* at MoMA PS 1, she's bald, earless, and armless. Her flayed cheeks are scored by raw, red-pink striations. Her chest and neck are made of something like Tinkertoys. A blue lattice juts from her throat. Is the purpose of such technology to repair or replace broken or missing parts and return the person to a normal level of functioning or is it to provide them with superhuman abilities? If this is the next stage in human evolution, I'll pass.

~~~~~

When I approach *Du, oder Ich?* a third time, I go slowly, looking, musing, and questioning. The woman in it is unmoved by my scrutiny.

I text a photo of the painting to my seventy-nine-year-old mother. "Oh, no!" she texts back. "Her body looks like mine!" I can hear the horror with which she'd say this. Later, while waiting for the A-Train in the subway, I show my twenty-four-year-old daughter the same photo. She, with her wild, glorious mop of curls, her short skirt, and cowboy boots assumes the woman's pose, one finger aimed at her temple, and one at me. Her impersonation isn't drastic or confrontational but cocky and funny. The world is her oyster.

But the woman's mien is dead serious. Her guns are loaded and cocked. One commentator suggested that because appreciation for Lassnig's work had been so slow in coming, in *Du, oder Ich* she was ready to shoot the viewer or herself. Another described Lassnig as "late flowering," which must have galled her as she'd been blooming all along. Perhaps she regretted not having children. Perhaps she regretted the diminishment and invisibility that accompanies aging in this youth-deifying time and place. I suspect that because she so seldom presented herself as happy, she must have felt that her sorrows and frustrations were the weightier, more provocative subject matter than her joys, delights, completeness, or contentment. But despite the adversity, it appears to me that Lassnig lived with gusto. If I were to paint a background for her, it would be a heap of cleaned-out oyster shells.

Lassnig mentioned boredom frequently enough that it must have been a strong motivating force in her life. "I can imagine going too far due to boredom (really going, to faraway valleys or countries), not finding your way back, not wanting to," she wrote in a journal entry. When Werneburg questioned her about this, she elaborated: "If nothing interests you anymore, you think you might as well die. I was recently in that situation again. But then someone came over and we talked and I was outside again." She also found release from boredom in a good movie. But even more, it was her explorations of her bodily sensations and various identities that saved her from despair—from pulling the trigger. "Es ist die Kunst, ja, ja, die macht mich immer jünger (...) Es ist die Kunst, die bringt mich nicht ins Grab," she sings in *Kantate*. "Yes, it's art that makes me younger and younger, it's art that prevents me from being driven into the grave."

On my fourth encounter with the painting, it strikes me that this outrageous woman might think she's being amusing. Surprise! The guns are loaded. Surprise! They're not. But I'm not laughing. In fact, I find her exasperating. "Du, oder Ich?" she croaks. Or is she cooing? If one of these guns weren't aimed at me, I'd ignore her. "You," I insist in hopes that I've called her bluff. "Not me. You." But she has no ears and so, she can't hear my answer. I've got to gesture my preference—fast.

Lassnig identified "*Du, oder Ich?*" as a "drastic" painting which, as she told Jorg Heiser in a 2006 interview in *frieze*, a British art journal, is a painting that tells a story as it "knock[s] truth on the head with a hammer." But what truth is she hammering in *Du, oder Ich?* When Lassnig was awarded the Golden Lions at age ninety-three, she remarked, perhaps with resignation, perhaps with resentment, perhaps with humor, "Too little too late." Is the hurt and frustration of such lately bestowed awards for a lifetime of extraordinary work (even in her eighties, she was a prolific, iconoclastic creative force) the reason she's brandishing those guns? Is she saying that now, with the added invisibility of agedness, she'll do whatever it takes to be seen?

In Lassnig's final years she depicted her feelings about her own aging, dying, and death. One of the most intriguing in this group is *Marked by Death* (2011), painted six years after *Du. oder Ich?* and three years before she died at ninety-four—which occurred, coincidentally, during the exhibit of her work at MoMA PS 1. Against a dark orange background, a pair of hands and wrists, joined by a cord, paint onto a white head Lassnig's upturned nose, closed eyes, small, triangular mouth, and ear. The German title of the painting at the MoMA exhibition is *Vom Tode Gezeichnet*, which means "marked by death," with "marked" meaning "the object of," a "sign, indication," as well as "importance, distinction." But in other exhibitions, the title of this painting is translated as "drawn by death," the translation I prefer. Lassnig is depicting herself as *drawn* or sketched by death; she is being *drawn* or attracted to death; she looks *drawn*, as in strained, pinched, or haggard by illness, exhaustion, or anxiety; she's *drawn* or pulled by death. While Lassnig is being marked or drawn by death, she's also the one creating, experiencing, and documenting it. Even as death approaches, she's curious, continuing to paint during all but the last few months of her life when she was deemed too frail to paint or to attend the exhibition at MoMA PS 1, where she and I might have met in the flesh, this woman who speaks to me about matters close to my heart: how to represent myself in my art; how I, who find it easier and more natural to think rather than feel, can become more attuned to what my body knows.

~~~~

When I approach the painting a final time, I view it from a greater distance. I wonder about the space between the woman's legs and what had been pulled out from under her. The bicycle that she rode the two hundred miles between her hometown of Klagenfurt to the art academy Vienna when she was twenty-two? A man or the men who had filled that space? Or was it her beloved motorcycle that she rode too fast, even in her later years?

With so many of Lassnig's self-portrayals, it's as if I've caught her in an unbecoming act. "When I'm painting, almost everything is allowed," she told Heiser. "Embarrassment is a challenge. I want to paint things that are uncomfortable." While most of us go out of our way to avoid embarrassing presentations of our self and the ridicule or rejection that can follow such exposure, Lassnig sought those situations and preserved them on canvas. In all her bizarre or macabre manifestations–herself as a dumpling, a lemon, a robot, a limbless Thalidomide-damaged body, a bare chest topped by a trachea topped by a vaginal opening surrounded by a triceratops's bony frill, a woman with bull horns and ears or with glob of brain bulging from the side of her head—she strikes me as excruciatingly self-aware. A "ruthless self-portraitist," art critic Gilda Williams called her. Embarrassment is a self-conscious state, dependent on an awareness of (or an anticipation of) the reactions of others. But Lassnig presents herself as almost always alone. Perhaps she's remembering a time when she felt awkward or ashamed about having been caught acting in a way that someone deemed as selfish or greedy or believing that she was invited or chosen when in fact, she wasn't, or when she was caught acting out a ritualized routine that she believed kept her safe. In some self-portraits, she seems, if not embarrassed, at least baffled by the unbecoming situation in which she finds herself. Or is she, through these various identities, not *unbecoming* but *becoming* (as in the process of passing into a different state) even more herself?

I could never stand so exposed before familiars and strangers showing them my gains and losses, demons and desires, so I admire Lassnig's vulnerability. Her act of baring herself (she reveals her eighty-five-year-old body without flinching, without apology) may be borne of despair (she has nothing to lose) or power (she has nothing to lose). Through self-exposure, she declares her power and autonomy. That is frightening. Liberating. Beautiful.

I confess that what I love most about Lassnig isn't her art but her indomitable spirit. Could I ever be as free as she is?

～～～

Once back home, I strip off my clothes in front of a full-length mirror and observe. How thin and bony I've become and how loose my flesh. But when I consider how well this body has served and continues to serve me, my pride and wonder are weightier than my embarrassment and sorrow.

I shut my eyes and look inward. My surroundings fade. My shoulders are hunched turtle-like from writing so many books and essays while bent over a keyboard. But as soon as I bring my awareness to them, my chest lifts and opens, uncaging my breath. I paint a pearl-gray bird flying from my mouth. My breasts which once were so much larger in my awareness—being looked at, admired, and touched, responding to touch, filling with and being emptied of milk—are now tiny, dry, and mute. I paint them powdery blue. A thin white scar marks the outer edge of the right one. I paint it like a zipper. My belly is paunchy, as if I'm several months pregnant. I paint it full of light and leaves. I depict my left hip and leg, which demand so little from me as a strong, graceful, shapely lavender column. Because a bicyclist slammed into me while I was walking on a biker-pedestrian path, my right hip, broken though technically "fixed," has a long pink-white seam running down the front of it and onto my thigh. The scar is rubbery and numb. In my mind's eye, my fake hip is bigger than the one my parents gave me. I depict it and my right thigh as packed with gray wool. The metal rods and bolts of my prosthesis demand my attention, since I can no longer move that hip naturally, freely, easily. I paint my right hip as a ratchet: solid, gray metal, mechanical, moving in stiff and predictable ways.

Other body parts swell and shrink, appear and disappear. Though my eyes are closed, I see them peering out beneath eyebrows that are all but gone and above smaller, lighter versions of the dark bags that my father carried beneath his eyes. Despite these changes, they're the same eyes that have always looked back at me, though milder—just as my fierce mother's eyes looked in her later years as her certainty and boldness faded. For my self-portrait, I'd paint four pairs of overlapping blue eyes, no two pairs alike. I consider titles for this view of myself. *Self-portrait: A Leg to Stand On. Self-portrait with a Dull Oyster Knife. Self-portrait: The Same Old Eyes.* Or simply, *Self-portrait #1*—the first of very many.

Name-staker

On the edge of a flower bed in the University of Nebraska's Yeutter
Garden, a man in a chartreuse vest studies a map, flips through a
three-ring binder containing photographs of plants, glances at the
map again. Then he pulls from a rack what looks like a weirdly
proportioned golf club or dental mirror. He drives the sharp
end of the club into the ground on the outer edge of a clump of
cranberry-pink blooms past their prime. When he steps back, I see
that the plaque atop the stake bears names: "Heartleaf-Bergenia/
Bergenia cordifolia." I consider these words. Because the edges of
the large, leathery leaves are rolled in, I can't see if they're heart
shaped. Bergenia. Probably the name of a botanist who studied
this plant. Is that with a hard or soft "g"? If it's the former, I'll see
reddish stems as assertively lifting the wilted blossoms above the
leaves. But if it's the latter, I'll see the stems as gently supporting
the blossoms. If I hadn't known the name of this plant, I might
have just glanced at the flowers and moved on, without noticing
the leaves or stalks, without searching for the right name for the
color of the petals, without considering the connections between
the name and the named.

Rather than continuing on to the library where I'd planned
to spend the afternoon reading student essays, I linger because
I'm enchanted by one revelation after another. The name-staker
doesn't seem to mind that I watch him work. Next to a cluster of
tall, elegant spikes of periwinkle-blue flowers with fused, sweet-
pea-like flowers, he drives a stake bearing the names "False Blue

Indigo/*Baptista australis.*" How could anything about this lovely, innocent plant be "false"? The names "Balloon Flower/*Platycodon grandiflorus*" are staked to a plant that, on this late May day, is nothing but leathery, blue-green, lance-shaped leaves and stems, which leaves me wondering about the aptness of the common name. But if I return mid-summer, I'll see the "balloons," poppable, light blue-violet orbs, that inspired the name.

I wouldn't need a chart to match some plants with their names. "Morning Light Silver Grass/*Miscanthis sinensis Rotsilber*" belongs to the fountain of grass with narrow, arching leaves, each streaked with bright silver. But other names prompt me to look closely for what inspired them. I like those names the best. I stand before a colony of "Solitary Clematis/*Clematis integrifolia.*" The four petals of this vivid blue-violet flower are puckered and slightly twisted. Together, they form a bell or urn, borne on a thin, wiry stem. How can the members of a colony be solitary? Yet on occasion, I have felt quite alone even when in a crowd of my own kind. What is the name for that experience? When I gently lift one of the nodding clematis blossoms and behold the stunning contrast of the bright yellow center against the deep, rich blue, my spirit swells and I gasp. What is the name for that response?

I'm distracted by a young couple leaving the university's Dairy Store, each carrying a waffle cone. They're a pretty pair, him with his green Bavarian Mint, her with her pink Raspberry Chocolate Chip. If I bought a scoop, I'd have a hard time choosing between Scarlet & Cream (vanilla ribboned with strawberries and straw-berry syrup) and Carmel Cashew (rich, shiny tan flecked with gold chunks). Could the man in chartreuse stake a name for this: my abrupt shift in focus following a span of rapt attention?

While I'm intrigued by the act of bestowing names and how a designation may or may not match the essence of that which it labels, I'm even more curious about those objects, organisms, experiences, and perceptions that bear no names. When I was ending my marriage, it struck me that to call the legal dissolution of the unions of those with and without children by the same name, "divorce," was to deny essential differences: that because the amount of time that a parent will have with his/her children is at stake, the effects of the dissolution might be particularly devastating; that though the legal marriage is over with the children, money, possessions, friends, and pets divvied up and the two parties gone to their separate addresses, the interactions between the former spouses will continue through their children's dance recitals, ball games, science fairs, graduations, and weddings and the dance recitals, ball games, science fairs, graduations, and weddings of their grandchildren. The dissolution of a childless marriage lacks these consequences. The different experiences of divorce call for different names.

Another stunning omission is the lack of a name for the parent whose child dies. A woman who loses her husband is called a widow. A man who loses a wife is called a widower. A child who loses their parents is called an orphan. The word "orphan" has been in use since about 1300 and "widow" is far older. But the lack of a name for the one who survives the death of his or her child is curious, since I've heard that described as the most grievous loss one can suffer. Does the lack of a name for this bereaved state hearken back to a time when most women gave birth every year or two, yet only a portion of their brood survived childhood, and so it was too risky to treasure one's offspring to the same extent that we do now, in this time of family planning, parenting experts, joint custody, and prolonged adolescence? Or is the omission primarily economic, since there are far fewer legal and economic ramifications from the death of a child than from that of a parent or spouse?

Noticing what isn't yet named is a contrary process, since it involves learning to see the unnoticed or unidentified. But I've found it to be a gratifying awareness to develop, since it expands the breadth of what I know and can articulate. Now I know that I want a name for the combination of remembered desire and current revulsion that arises in me as I watch my cat pummel the comforter on my bed as if it were bread dough or aching muscles. I want a name for that point in my grieving when I started dreaming of my beloved dead in such a way that I felt accompanied and comforted all day and believed, really believed, that there are more painful forms of separation than death. I want a name for that transitional state following my arrival home from a long trip when, even though I'm sitting in my living room in my favorite spot, sipping tea from my favorite mug, that which governs my sense of movement and stasis is still in motion, still traveling. I want a name for that type of conversation that I've had a few dozen times in my life, in which the talk is so deep, soulful, intimate, and revelatory that the other conversers and I are not aware of time's swift passage and the gathering darkness or approaching dawn, until something breaks in—the crying child, the knock on the door, the closing call—and yanks us back into ordinary time and talk.

Nassim Nicholas Taleb, the author of *Antifragile: Things that Gain from Disorder*, filled an emptiness by coining a name for a counterintuitive process that he observed and studied. Taleb says that "some things benefit from shocks; they thrive and grow when exposed to volatility, randomness, disorder, and stressors and love, adventure, risk, and uncertainty." Yet despite the ubiquity of this phenomenon, there was no word for the opposite of fragile. Talib says that what he calls the "antifragile" is "beyond resilience or robustness. The resilient resists shocks and stays the same; the antifragile gets better." To illustrate, he points to the Hydra, the mythological, many-headed sea monster. Each time Hercules cut off one of the Hydra's heads, two more sprang forth. Because the Hydra used trauma and adversity as the impetus for growth, the creature was antifragile.

Taleb, a Professor of Risk Engineering at New York University's Polytechnic Institute, says that in recent decades, our society has created conditions that while providing us with the illusion of safety, have also "fragiliz[ed] the economy, our health, political life, education, almost everything . . . by suppressing randomness and volatility." The New York banking system, five banks, each too big to fail, is an example of extreme fragility, since the failure of one bank threatens the entire system; bailouts make the system even more fragile, since the learning and adjustments that could result from a bank closure can't happen. In contrast, the restaurant sector, comprised of many, many establishments of various sizes, styles, and philosophies, is robust because the failure of one restaurant doesn't jeopardize the others. And, too, the restaurant sector as a whole is antifragile because other restaurants learn and improve after observing the mistakes made by those that went out of business. A fragile education is one in which the children are overprogrammed, overscheduled, and overprotected, and so, not permitted to make the kind of mistakes that would allow them to develop strength and resilience. A robust education is one based on the chaotic and unpredictable nature of "street life"; an antifragile education is one of street fights and unlimited access to a good parental library. Taleb summarizes: "Skills that transfer: street fights, off-path hiking, seduction, broad erudition. Skills that don't: school, games, sports, laboratory—what's reduced and organized."

I, too, have coined terms and have created new uses for existing words. The one that has gained the widest currency is "perhapsing," a term I created to describe the speculation or conjecture that I engage in when I don't have all the information I need to flesh out a passage in one of my essays. As a writer of creative nonfiction, it would be unethical for me to fictionalize. But if I inform my readers that the information I'm including is speculative rather than fact-based through such words and phrases as *perhaps, maybe, possibly,* or *could have been,* I'm on firm ethical ground. Then, if my memory of the time that I learned a secret is fuzzy and incomplete, I can "perhaps" details and plausible dialogue. Then if the person I'm profiling can't or won't speak of what it was like to grow up in a good-hearted but flawed utopian community, I can "perhaps" likely reasons.

Increasingly, I find myself in need of words to name my experiences with aging, the new land through which I'm journeying. While I occasionally hear travelers' tales about the beautiful harbors, fertile valleys, and welcoming, energizing cities in this land, the most readily available maps of the place were drawn by sojourners whose paths wound through spartan, hardscrabble landscapes and ended at waste dumps or dead ends. I don't want to follow in their footsteps. While I yearn for maps on which the landmarks, boundaries, mileage posts, and detours are well marked, and while I yearn for signs announcing what's ahead ("Blind curve!" or "Here be dragons!" or "Healing water below!"), I'm charting my own course, naming what I find as I go.

One experience that I need a name for is the habit of describing an attractive, vibrant, older person as "looking ten years younger" than their chronological age or being "young at heart" or thinking or acting "more progressively" or "decades younger" than you'd expect. What these statements reveal is that the beholder and their culture have a limited and limiting view of what is possible for an older person. Why can't a nonagenarian be fit, supple, vibrant, and dynamic? Why is a young heart better than a big, old, wise heart, practiced in the ways of love, loss, passion, forgiveness, and generosity?

Another experience I need a name for is the blessed aversion I've felt since my early fifties toward some things for which I used to have a hearty appetite. For instance, I have no desire to attend another writing conference, even if it is in Iceland or Australia, Seattle or Tampa, or to tour another Midwestern Danish, German, Czech, Dutch, or Swedish heritage museum, or read another memoir about finding home. Once I let go of what no longer nourishes me (not easy, since I'm loyal and resist change), I can, in the newly opened spaces and with the newly available energy, devote myself to more relevant, zestier, and satisfying passions.

Now I, for whom work often came above all else for so long, will cheerfully and with only a smidgen of guilt clear my schedule so I can spend time with friends or family or volunteering. Now I, who for decades wrote about the human and natural history of Iowa and Nebraska, the two places I call home, and how people shape or are shaped by the land, have turned from that once enlivening but now lackluster subject to one that I find more energizing and meaningful: the relationships between and among people; how we shape or are shaped by culture.

So, too, I need a name for an experience of which I've become keenly aware: when a brief glance simultaneously renders an older person highly visible (one's agedness is all that the beholder sees) and largely invisible (no matter how saucy, buff, visionary, icon-oclastic, or buzzing with energy one is, no matter how much wisdom, love, truth, or grace one embodies, one's agedness is all that the beholder sees). While the person who cannot see is the one with the deficiency, the one who has been invisibilized feels that they are the one who is wanting and so, unworthy of regard.

In mythology and literature, the man (it's always a male) who donned the cape or helmet of invisibility is endowed with super-human powers that could be used for good or ill: while invisible, Perseus escaped from the vengeful sisters of Medusa, who he'd just killed; while invisible, the soldier in the Grimm fairy tale "The Twelve Dancing Princesses" discovered where the lovely sisters went each night in defiance of their father, the king; while invisible, Dr. Griffin in H. G. Wells's novel *The Invisible Man* robbed and murdered. While the growing invisibility that accompanies aging is generally disempowering, it isn't without benefits for some. When she turned fifty, Carolyn C. Heilbrun, a feminist scholar and author of detective novels, said she would have made the ideal burglar since no one could see her anymore. In *The Change: Women, Aging, and Menopause* (1993), Germaine Greer claims that invisibility is desirable because finally, the older woman can "transcend the body that was what other people principally valued her for, and be set free both from their expectations and her own capitulation to them." Greer's view needs to be contextualized. She has long been in the public eye as one of the most significant and controversial feminist voices of the twentieth century. Perhaps after decades of being noticed, she felt relief in becoming less conspicuous as she aged. But it's not relief that most of my over-fifty friends and I feel about our invisibility; rather, we feel sad, frustrated, and undermined.

When we fail to bring into words our experiences and concepts because they conflict with our professed values or point to something we'd rather not acknowledge, we render our experiences mute and impotent. The effects of that are disabling, dangerous even. Any of us who live long enough in this youth-worshipping culture will be invisibilized by our juniors, but without the words to speak of that common experience, we won't be fully aware of when and why it's happening, how we feel when it happens, and what to do about it. When I read Margaret Cruikshank's 2009 *Learning to be Old: Gender, Culture, and Aging*, I acquired some of the language and concepts I needed to describe my experience of aging and to inform the way I approach it. Cruikshank says that we have to "learn" to be old, to "inhabit" our age, to "perform" our agedness: "An old woman becomes old not by any words or gestures, necessarily, but by having projected onto her [the] younger women's culturally-shaped notions of what old is." Chief among these values is that the old don't merit being seen and regarded. Too many of us older women voluntarily, or perhaps with a little persuasion or coercion, wrap ourselves in the cape of invisibility that society has fashioned for us. Yet if the way we express our age is determined more by culture than biology, then we have choices as to how we inhabit or perform our age.

The name-staker at the Yeutter Garden works with plants in the berms and rock garden that already bear layers of names. His job is simply to match the name to the plant to which it belongs. But my task of staking my unnamed experiences is more demanding. To prepare myself, I read lyric essays so that my head is full of compressed, precise, dazzling language and associative leaps. I read the works of age theorists like Kathleen Woodward, Simone de Beauvoir, and Margaret Morganroth Gullette, as well as Cruikshank, Heilbrun, and Greer so that I'm sensitized and defiant. I recognize and delineate my perceptions and feelings and talk to perceptive others about theirs. Then, I begin naming what grows in my garden.

"Age passing" is what I choose to call the acts of one who invests time, money, creativity, and energy in disguising themselves as a younger person and to avoid being overlooked, in both senses of that contranym (watched closely from above; deliberately disregarded or ignored) Passing, according to Wikipedia, "is the ability of a person to be regarded as a member of social groups other than his or her own, such as a different race, ethnicity, caste, social class, gender, age and/or disability status, generally with the purpose of gaining social acceptance or to cope with difference anxiety." I quote this definition only because every item listed is blue and hyperlinked *except* for age—the stage in life for which we have the least adequate vocabulary, the stage in life that will affect everyone who lives long enough. Dying your gray hair black or blond and spending hours at the gym each day to give your body a shape that is more angular than round might make you feel more secure about keeping your job and your boyfriend, yet the gains are offset by the losses of not being able to set photos of your teenaged grandchildren on your desk at work or telling anecdotes about your thirtieth or fortieth high school reunion or eating lunch with the other older employees who are chatting about that great article in the most recent issue of AARP *The Magazine* about how to get along with your young boss for fear of appearing old and out of the loop. Because of the greater distance between your real and your perceived identity, "age passing" makes you vulnerable, susceptible, and fragile. One revealing or uncensored moment (when it's your turn to talk at the meeting, you flush bright red and break a sweat because of a hot flash; when you receive news that you won the grant you applied for, you exclaim, "Now we're cooking with gas!"), and the jig is up.

I call those who encourage and praise people who are "age passing" as younger than their years "age disclaimers," since they deny or repudiate the full range of what is possible in older people. The author of an article on a pop culture website was "disclaiming" when she wrote that sixty-seven-year-old Helen Mirren is "forever *frozen* as a classy, regal woman of 50" (italics are mine). Gloria Steinem was "claiming" when, on her fortieth birthday, she said, "This is what forty looks like—we've been lying for so long, who would know?" Steinem's friend Robin Morgan was also "claiming" when instead of saying that at eighty, Steinem has the energy, power, and drive of one several decades younger, that at eighty, her friend is "a better organizer . . . a better persuader . . . a better writer than she ever has been." Disclaiming one's true age (sixty is the new fifty) is dishonest and thwarting; claiming one's true age (sixty is sixty) is honest and liberating.

"Afternooning" is what I call the weariness, boredom, or ennui I feel toward what held my attention when I was younger and using that newly released time, energy, and creativity for activities that I now find more vibrant and fulfilling. In a 1933 essay, "The Stages of Life," psychotherapist Carl G. Jung observed that during middle age, what he called "the afternoon of life," one cannot live "according to the program of life's morning—for what was great in the morning will be little at evening, and what in the morning was true will at evening have become a lie." Middle age, the afternoon of life, is just as meaningful as the morning; yet its meaning and purpose are different. This letting go or shaking off what once gripped one's attention and embracing the new and more consequential is vital since, as Jung says, middle age has "significance of its own and cannot merely be a pitiful appendage to life's morning." During the afternoon of life, we can develop those parts of ourselves that we ignored or postponed attending to when we were younger. Thus, the one who long sought personal success, power, and approval in the marketplace, craves time at home, playing with the grandchildren, making and eating slow, homemade lunches, reading those books that one never had time for before, and never again wearing makeup and uncomfortable-but-stylish shoes. One who devoted decades to creating harmony, order, and abundance in the domestic sphere is wild to be out in the public sphere, honing one's leadership skills, commanding audiences, eating fast lunches on the go, never again sitting in the back corner as one seeks to create harmony, order, and abundance in one's city, country, world. Both are afternooners. By balancing and integrating their hungers and surfeits, their strengths and weaknesses, both types are becoming less fragile, more robust, even antifragile.

My chosen names for the act of being rendered invisible because of my age or of my invisiblizing others because of their age is inspired by the 2014 invention of an invisibility cape. The "Rochester Cloak," so called because it was invented at the University of Rochester in New York, isn't really a cape but a physical structure that hides from view both the obscuring device and what that lies behind it. The cloak consists of four carefully placed standard lenses (they look like magnifying glasses to me) of the correct power, spaced the correct distance apart in terms of focal lengths, and held in place by an optical bench. The two outer lenses focus the light from a wide area onto the two smaller lenses in the middle, which creates a region where the incident light can't reach the object, and the reflective light can't reach the beholder. To make a pencil disappear, you place it between the first two lenses. Then when you look through the lenses, what you see isn't the pencil but what's beyond the farthest lens, the picture on the wall. The Rochester Cloak doesn't create transparency; rather it guides light around the obscuring object, so that the object you want to hide isn't visible. Optical cloaking, it's called. The photograph accompanying the article from the University of Rochester News

Center about this invention shows a man holding a lens before his right eye. I had to look at the photo again before I realized that where the man's eye socket should have been is the picture on the wall behind him. "Invisibilized" and "invisibilizing" are fine terms, but I prefer the simplicity of "cloaking" and "cloaked" for this phenomenon because they suggest, in concrete terms, the illness (cloaking another or being cloaked) and the cure (refusing to cloak or be cloaked).

Usually, I'm not aware that I've wrapped myself in an invisibility cloak, or more likely, that one has been thrown over me, until I realize that even though I'm standing directly in front of someone, they're looking past me, as if there are four lenses between us bending light rays around me, concealing my softly creased face, the gray hairs among the blonde, my direct, unwavering gaze, my yoga-supple spine, joints, tendons, and spirit, and the wisdom and experience I've gained over many decades. Also, I've had to learn to see the cloaks that I've thrown on others, something I do with far less frequency than I used to now that I know how it feels.

Now, when I encounter someone who is "age passing," "afternooning," "cloaking," "being cloaked," "disclaiming," or "being disclaimed," I slip the name for the phenomenon into my conversation with them. If I see a look of perplexity flash across their face, I define the term and provide examples. While my hopes are lofty (I want these neologisms to catch on and cause a revolution in how we see and respond to aging), what is of more immediate concern to me is that I remember these terms when I'm sad, angry, or rattled about having been cloaked or disclaimed and want to name and challenge rather than run and hide from the affront.

When I return to Yeutter Garden in early July, the name-staker is gone. The garden is crowded with flowers and foliage that grow so quickly in the heat. People stroll along the paths on the edges of the flower beds, marveling at the lilies, balloon flowers, speedwells, hawkweeds, coreopsis, harebells, bees, and butterflies, and reading the names on the plaques. The blossoms of the Heart-leaf

Bergenia are gone, but the large, shaggy, brilliant red-orange flower heads of "Gardenview Scarlet Bee Balm/*Monarda didyma*" are in full and luscious bloom, as are the lovely, airy blossoms of the Balloon Flower. Every plant is staked and named; every plant is worthy of consideration. Yet it occurs to me that I should look again, since there might be something growing here that I can't see because it hasn't yet been named and staked.

Broom Dance

I push the button and horns blare. After a few bars, Ella Fitzgerald's lush, supple voice fills the room: "You are the promised kiss of springtime / That makes the lonely winter seem long." I grab the broom from behind the kitchen door and flip it so that I am face-to-face with its plastic bristles. I feel the beat, five-six-seven-eight, and then step back with my right foot—slow, slow, quick, quick. In my ballroom dance class, the teacher tells us that the "girl" is to look over the "guy's" left shoulder as she glides backward, confident that he's wisely, safely leading them. Whether it's new or familiar terrain that he's chosen for them to enter, she does so blindly, trustingly. But as my plastic dance partner stiffly guides me through the kitchen and into the dining room, I peak over my shoulder, so I don't step on a cat or run into furniture.

"I want everyone to practice the foxtrot this week," Stacey said before we left class last Monday evening. When her eyes landed on me, unpartnered and by far the oldest person in the class, she curtly added, "You can practice with a broom." My carefully plaited dignity raveled, and I blushed. I wondered if the others in dance class were pitying me as they pictured me with no one to dance with but a broom. Or maybe because I'm decades older than them, they gave no thought to me and how I lived.

Stacey's suggestion didn't surprise me. While she is a skilled and inspired teacher, when she demonstrates new steps or variations, she says things like, "I'm wearing a dress today, so I'll be the girl." Or "Ladies! I want you to learn both the girl's and the guy's parts. But never," she paused, "take the lead away from him." This Nebraska farm girl turned successful businesswoman has labeled the restrooms in her studio, bar, and ballroom "Guys" and "Dolls." She encourages the "ladies" in the class to purchase the sparkly, strappy, back- and knee-stressing high-heeled dance shoes that she sells. I haven't seen the lesbian couple since the third class.

Everyone in Ballroom 100 at the Riviera Ballroom enrolled as a couple except for Zach and me. In fact, several of the couples are preparing for wedding dances. Zach and his woman friend signed up for the class together, but she parted ways with him before the first session. Because of Stacey's "no refund policy," Zach also comes to class alone. He and I are dance partners.

The no refund policy is why I'm there, too. For my birthday, my daughter enrolled me in an eight-week dance class. "A potted azalea or a pair of earrings would have been just fine," I told her. "Can you return this?" "Nope," she said. "I paid a lot of money for that class. You have to go three times before you can quit." But much to my surprise, I like going to class in the hip part of the city where parking is scarce even on a Monday evening, like learning something utterly new, like dancing with a sweet guy twenty-five years younger than me, like foxtrotting, waltzing, or tangoing to Frank Sinatra, Michael Bublé, and various versions of "La Cumparsita," music I'd never listen to otherwise. In truth, I've always wanted to learn to dance. In my imagination I see myself dancing with grace, fluidity, and confidence. Sometimes in class, I forget my self-consciousness and my conviction that I can't do this unless I'm watching Zach's feet. Then I lift my head, and we sail around the room: slow, slow, quick, quick, and an easy promenade.

When the broom and I can go no further in the dining room without my "taillights," as Stacey calls them, hitting a chair, we do a box step rotation. Fitzgerald begins a new song: "I thought I'd found the man of my dreams / Now it seems, this is how the story ends." My partner and I head for the living room.

Stacey could have simply told me to practice the steps, as she did Zach. Or she could have told me to dance with something else—a hoe, a closed umbrella, or a teddy bear. Yet none of those are as freighted with significance as a common, humble broom with its phallic handle, the female energies associated with the round bundle of twigs of an old-time besom, and its long links with domesticity, ritual, and power. While most broom makers in Europe were male, woman also collected bundles of stiff reeds, twigs, or husks and tied them to a stick. The female speaker in the eighteenth-century British folk song, "The Besom Maker" says of her work: "Sweet pleasure I enjoy, both morning, night and noon, / Going over the hills so high a-gathering of green broom." After the baby arrives, she says that she'll "bundle up my besoms and take them to the fair / And sell them all by wholesale, nursing's now my care."

It was the celibate Shakers who turned the round brooms of Europe into the flat brooms of North America to produce a broader path as they swept crumbs and ashes from the floors of their houses and by extension, their hearts and souls. The Shakers were also known for their unharmonized, unaccompanied singing and the stomping movements of their narrow-patterned group dances in which the male and female participants never touched. As their movements drew them closer to God, they became so ecstatic that they would "shake" and speak in tongues. But perhaps when no one else was around, a Shaker woman experienced a different type of joy, when, like Disney's Cinderella, she danced not as she was taught, but freestyle with her broom, moving in whatever way felt right in that ripe moment.

Witches also "danced" with their brooms. Some believe that this practice developed from an ancient pagan tradition in which people mounted on pitchforks, poles, and brooms leapt as high as they could over their seeded fields in order to raise the crops or to persuade the gods to bless the harvest. Witches, with their heretical ideas about female empowerment and how and where that power came from, found that plants like henbane, mandrake, jimsonweed, and deadly nightshade gave them vivid flight dreams. Yet when taken orally, these herbs caused nasty side effects ("Hot as a hare, red as a beet, dry as a bone, blind as a bat, mad as a hatter" are the symptoms of anticholinergic syndrome) and sometimes death. In his *Book of Poisons*, German toxicologist Gustav Schenk reports that when he took henbane, "My teeth were clenched, and a dizzied rage took possession of me." But, too, he knew that he was "permeated by a peculiar sense of well-being connected with the crazy sensation that my feet were growing lighter, expanding and breaking loose from my own body." Then, he was "seized with the fear that I was falling apart. At the same time, I experienced an intoxicating sensation of flying." As a safer way of administering their flying potions, witches mixed a salve of hallucinogenic herbs and animal fat and applied it with a broom-stick to their sweat glands and mucous membranes. Or they rode broomsticks that they'd slathered with flying ointment into the wild blue yonder. If Cinderella had never met the prince, what different version of "happily ever after" might she have known through her broom dances?

In the wide, open spaces of my living room, I inform my plastic dance partner that we're switching roles. I've never led, so the act feels wrong, then defiant, then thrilling as I step forward with my left foot. My partner stares blankly over my shoulder; but I see everything. We circle the room; we take a swaggy, leisurely promenade around the coffee table, around the rocking chair, and back. After Fitzgerald finishes singing "Can't We Be Friends?" we pause in the silence. A blast of horns is followed by a long, silvery scat. *Eee da bee doo dah dah daah. Bo dah dad a door. Ya dah dah dahdahdahdah dah.* This music is not made for patterned dances like those that I learned at the Riviera Ballroom, so as we wait, I sway. Finally, Fitzgerald sings. "Blue skies smiling at me / Nothing but blue skies do I see," and my partner and I glide around the room. The beat is bright and bouncy. At the chorus, Fitzgerald is behind the beat; then, she steps out in front. To create the feel of shifting, syncopated meters, she replaces two groups of three beats with three groups of two beats. She calls to the trumpets and they answer. The tinkling piano strolls along behind her as the cymbals softly shuffle. Fitzgerald's next scat—*Be doo doo be doooo. Duh ya duh ya. Eeee. Bom boom bah dee. Dee dah-yowww. Sssss. Nahnahnaaeeeya. Dahdahloobah*—is too wild and virtuosic for foxtrotting and too euphoric for me to listen to without moving. I toss my partner aside. I swirl and undulate. I'm light-footed. I leap into the air. I leap again, longer, higher, face first. I glide above the treetops; I skirt towers. I cruise through time zones, dodging jets and hot-air balloons, hailing other broom dancers, and racing white-hot meteors before my feet touch earth again.

Faith, Bone Deep

Three years ago a bone density test revealed that I had osteopenia, a lower-than-normal bone mineral density. But the radiologist who read my more recent scan found "a worsening of bone mass density" in my lumbar spine. In other words, over the past three years, I've developed larger holes or spaces in my bone tissue. Using the Fracture Assessment Risk Tool (FRAX), the radiologist calculated that my "ten-year probability of a major osteoporotic fracture is 11% and of hip fracture, 2.5%." I question the accuracy of this tool, since it didn't consider when predicting my future factors such as my diet, exercise regimen, medical history, and mindset. Even so, it seemed prudent for me to take the projection seriously and strengthen my porous bones.

And yet, there was something in this diagnosis that I didn't want to take to heart. While I was concerned about the threat to health, longevity, and autonomy that "a major osteoporotic fracture" can cause, I was struck that much of what I learned about my disease felt like a character judgment—as if my foundation was too rickety to support a vibrant, worthwhile life; as if instead of standing up to my full height, I was cowering; as if with my spongy hip bones, I hadn't a good leg to stand on; as if lazy, selfish, spineless me hadn't borne the load, carried my weight, or been tough enough when facing stress and travail. In a structural and elemental sense, I hadn't measured up and now it was time for me to pay. Since what we're told to believe about ourselves can become what we hold as true which in turn shapes our reality, I regretted the judgments that this diagnosis imparted.

To slow the speed of resorption, the process by which osteoclasts, a type of bone cell, break down bone tissue and release the minerals into the blood, my doctor recommended that I take a bisphosphonate for five years. But my research revealed that this pharmaceutical response to my malady had questionable results. For instance, in a study published in the June 2024 issue of the *American Journal of Medicine*, Dr. Christopher W. Goodman writes that an analysis of the clinical research underlying the recommendation that bisphosphonates be the "first-line therapy" for osteoporosis by the American College of Physicians, the U.S. Preventive Services Task Force, and other groups reveals that the supporting evidence is "narrower and less certain than described in clinical guidelines." Even if this class of drugs was reasonably effective, the more common side effects like irritation, perforation, or ulcers of the esophagus; a rapid or irregular heart rate; inflammatory eye disease; and joint, bone, and muscle pain, as well as rarer but more alarming ones, such as esophageal cancer, low impact factures of the thighbone, renal failure, and jawbone necrosis, give me serious pause about taking such chemicals into my body. And, too, a broken bone might be slower to heal if one has taken a bisphosphonate long-term, as I was being advised to do, than if one hasn't. Only as a last resort would I take this or one of the other osteoporosis drugs, which also had dubious results and troubling side effects. So, that left exercise. Not the walking, yoga, and upper body work with light, handheld weights that I'd done for decades, but weight-bearing exercise that was rigorous enough to build bones and muscles. More work. More burdens. More resistance. More impact. I was heartened by what I read about weight-bearing exercise as a remedy for osteoporosis, since it had proven benefits and no dangers—unless one did it wrong. My doctor supported my desire to treat my condition with exercise, as long as I was willing to work hard. After one year, we'd retest and make a treatment decision based on the new results. I was willing.

~~~~~~

I've never met a tree that I didn't like. So whether I'm strolling in my neighborhood or hiking at the nature center, I take notice and tip my hat to them. In the warmer, more light-filled part of the year, leafed, flowered, or fruited trees are easy to love and identify. But I also appreciate winter trees because in them, I can more easily see their structure or skeleton, and I enjoy the challenge of identifying them by their silhouette, bark, and buds. And without the leaves, it's easier to observe who else is there. If I'm walking at dusk in the colder, darker part of the year, I pause to watch squirrels crawl into messy nests held aloft or peering out of knotholes; rattling northern flickers drumming for insects in decaying wood; perched red-tailed hawks keeping a close eye on me. But any time of year, I'm drawn to the stark beauty of dying or dead trees: a branch, snapped, caught, and dangling from a fork in another branch; peeling bark; bare fingery branchlets rising above leafy lower ones; jagged tears on the trunk and limb where insects, fungi, and bacteria enter and turn wood into life-nourishing soil; old bones creaking in the wind.

~~~~~~

Vrksasana (tree pose) is a yoga posture I've been practicing for over forty years. But never with gusto. In fact, I long thought it a waste of time. Give me the quadriceps burn of Virabhadrasana I, II, and III (the warrior poses), the gluteal contraction of Utkatasana (chair pose), the intense front body stretch of Urdva Dhanuarasa (upward facing bow pose), or the spinal torsion of Ardha Matsyendrasana (Half Lord of the Fishes Pose). But Tree Pose? It demanded little and gave little in return. When I did practice it, which wasn't often, I tried to be grateful for what it could teach me about patience, balance, and the suspension of judgment.

To practice Vrksasana, enter through Tadasana (mountain pose), the basic standing pose. Bend one knee and place that foot on the inner thigh of your standing leg, as close to your groin as possible. If you can't place your foot that high on your thigh, place it lower on your leg. Press into the floor the four points of your standing foot (two in the heal; one each beneath the big and pinky toes). Turn out the knee on your standing leg. So that you don't waver or fall, focus on a spot on the wall. Open your hips. Balance them so that they're level and not leaning toward your standing leg. Lift and open your chest. Clasp your hands at your heart or overhead in prayer position. Breathe smoothly and fully.

In the first frame of a chart illustrating the four stages of osteoporosis, the woman has no noticeable symptoms: her spine and posture appear normal—as do mine. In the second, there's a rounding of her shoulders, a slight humping of her back, and jutting forward of her neck. In the third, each of these movements is more pronounced. In the fourth, she's so badly stooped she leans on a cane, and her head projects far enough forward that I don't know how she swallows food or looks anyone in the eye. What's most unsettling are the growing number of fractures in her lumbar and thoracic spine over the four frames. These compressions are shown in hot red.

The most likely cause of her thinning bones is aging. But other causes, none of which a DEXA scan reveals, include high thyroid, parathyroid, or adrenal hormonal levels; low estrogen; rheumatoid arthritis; and gastrointestinal issues that affect absorption of vitamin and minerals, including celiac disease, Irritable Bowel Syndrome, Crohn's disease, and Small Intestine Bacterial Overgrowth—the last, a condition I have. My mother, who drank too much alcohol and took a steroid for her asthma for several years, both of which decrease bone density, had osteopenia. Her mother took a disturbing number of prescription and nonprescription drugs for most of her life. That, too, is a risk factor. Her osteoporosis was so bad that she wore a contraption on her collapsing chest to maintain distance between her chin and belly. With or without this support, she looked miserable. Neither woman had ever exercised, also a risk factor. My bone-weakening "addiction" is an eating disorder that seized me when I was in my teens and again in my mid-twenties, kept its distance while I was raising my children, but recaptured me at the start of menopause and seems unwilling to make a full retreat. Not eating well or enough is also a risk factor for osteoporosis.

But I've made changes. Since building muscle strengthens bones and muscles need protein to grow or at least to not lose mass, I've doubled my protein consumption. I achieved this in part by ending my forty-year commitment to vegetarianism and becoming a pescatarian. I don't eat sardines and anchovies for the calcium and vitamin D, since there's no conclusive evidence in the studies I've read in medical journals that either nutrient prevents fractures, a fact which astounded me. In one study, published in the venerable, peer-reviewed *British Medical Journal* in 2015, researchers analyzed 120 systemic reviews or meta-analyses that examined the link between calcium intake and bone mineral density. They concluded that neither dietary nor supplemental calcium prevents fractures and so advised that "clinicians, advocacy organisations, and health policymakers" stop recommending that people increase their calcium intake either through supplements or dietary sources to prevent fractures. Likewise, a 2022 Harvard Medical School study resoundingly rejects the claim that vitamin D improves bone density in healthy middle-aged and older adults, since they found it to be no more effective in doing so than a placebo. Yet my doctor, a smart, young, Mayo-trained internist, who I adore, advised that each day I exceed the recommended daily allowances of calcium for a woman my age by a couple hundred milligrams and to take several thousand international units of vitamin D. Most days I follow his advice. While calcium and vitamin D won't heal my bones, a deficit of either of those vital nutrients would weaken them. The real reason I now eat tiny fish is because of the homeopathic principle "Let like be treated by likes." Their oily, supple, delicate spines will feed my dry, brittle, porous one.

Strength and vitality are what I want, but achieving these through exercise is harder than I expected. Just fifteen minutes into the Fit for Life class at the YMCA, all my joints, with the curious exception of my left hip and knee, ached. Water fitness, a decent cardio workout and muscle-builder that's easier on the joints, isn't recommended by the National Osteoporosis Association since it isn't a weight-bearing exercise and so can't increase bone density. Though I enjoyed the camaraderie and levity of the participants in both classes and that those who go for coffee afterward invited me to join them, I didn't continue either. When I walked several miles carrying six pounds in my weighted vest, my right hip and knee ached so badly that I could only do a minimal workout for the next several days. I still walk with my vest, though I'm embarrassingly far from the ten pounds that my doctor prescribed. Despite a rotator cuff injury in both shoulders which keeps me from working my upper body as vigorously as I'd like, each morning I follow along with YouTube videos—Pilates for Osteoporosis, Man Flow Yoga for bone strength, and exercises with the Brick House Bones physical therapist. My favorite guide, the Yoga for Osteoporosis teacher, makes Tree Pose harder for her viewers. Instead of spotting so that we're steady, she directs us to move our eyes from side to side so we're constantly readjusting, using the muscles along our spine, the sides of our hips, and in our core to steady ourselves so that we don't wobble or topple. With this adaptation, Vrksasana is a challenging, balance- and muscle-building posture that I'm growing to respect.

I see the results of my hard work in my core, glutes, and quadriceps, which are stronger and shapelier than they used to be; my upper body is also gaining strength, though not as quickly or as dramatically. But I don't yet know if I'm doing enough to coun-

teract the effects of aging and my "cushy" life and so, to change
the ratio of substance to space in my bones.

~~~~~

A silver maple that I often pass on my neighborhood rambles is
leafed out on the bottom limbs while those at the top are bare. A
dead branch hooked in the fork of another hangs perilously; above
it, an even larger branch is caught in a higher crook. I won't walk
beneath them, since either is big enough to cause brain damage
should they drop on my head. But from a distance, I stop and drop
my head back, so I can admire the bone-white, bone-smooth, bar-
kless branches; the branchlets veining the sky; the delicate balance
of the dangling branches swaying in the breeze like kinetic art.

Silver maples, also called "soft" or "water" maples, aren't fussy.
They grow just about anywhere there's enough water. Because
they grow quickly and their roots are shallow, they're less able
than the hardwoods to resist the trauma and decay caused by
lightning strikes, strong winds, or disease. Likewise, old, porous
bones are more likely than younger, denser ones to fracture if,
with a concave spine, you lift a crockpot full of soup or trip and
fall while trying not to step on the cat.

A chart from the Arbor Day Foundation presents the life of
a deciduous tree in seven stages. In infancy, the tree is tiny and
vulnerable; in youth, its branches are slender and come to a peak
on top. A tree in the prime of its life has a round crown filled with
long, strong branches. In middle age, the limbs grow thicker and
heavier, producing a flatter crown with wide, generous shade. A
"senior" tree has gaps in the canopy where large limbs once rose;
the remaining ones might host suckers. We tend to trees at this
stage of life by watching and treating for insects and diseases.
When trees are in their "twilight," like the silver maple I visit on
my neighborhood rambles, their big limbs die and break, leaving an even smaller, more open crown, spottier shade, and more
suckers. To keep people, properties, and other branches safe, we

must remove dead limbs—like the danglers on the silver maple in my neighborhood—and continue monitoring and treating for wood-weakening invaders. The twilight phase can last as long as a half century. The final stage is death, when even the strongest and best cared for tree falls or must be felled.

The trees that broke in the windstorm last summer were a tragedy. But the decline of this elderly silver maple that I sometimes pass on my many and various neighborhood rambles is a softer sadness. Though the decline and death of trees is a natural, normal process, I grieve a bit when I see it happening. And, too, it reminds me that weakening, thinning bones and branches is a natural, normal process—in trees, dogs, mice, pigs, pigeons, and people who live long enough.

Vrksasana is one of the most ancient yoga postures. A seventh- or eighth-century stone carving in Mahabalipuram Shore Temple on India's east coast depicts a bearded, loin-clothed yogi, probably Arjuna, Krishna's student and the hero of the Hindu epic *Mahabharata*, who is so emaciated that every rib in his bare chest is outstanding and his abdomen concave. He stands on one leg with his hands pressed in prayer pose above his head. Even the most casual Y or rec center yoga student would recognize this as tree pose. The gaunt man's practice of the posture isn't like that of B. K. S. Iyengar, whose execution of the asanas is, in my mind, as close to perfection as anyone can get. In the photo accompanying his description of Vrksasana in *Light on Yoga* (1966), Iyengar creates, with his heel at his groin, bent knee pointing down, hips balanced, chest broad, and shoulders so open that his extended upper arms are behind his head, a mighty, towering, and tapered tree. But the Mahabalipuram yogi rests his foot below his knee instead of at the groin, so his knee points out instead of earthward; he's lifted his arms overhead, but they're soft and crooked at the elbows, creating a rounded rather than peaked canopy. His eyes are closed and his face loose, suggesting that he's deep in meditation or absorbed in the chanting of his mantra. He doesn't care one whit what I think of him, his practice, or his version of tree pose.

~~~~~

Louise Hay, the author of *You Can Heal Your Life* (1984), says that the psychospiritual causes of disease and disfunction are far weightier than the biological factors. She identifies the "probable cause" of osteoporosis as the feeling that "there is no support left in life." Since any disease is a stew of biological, genetic, environmental, cultural, and emotional factors, Hay is partially right. Age has narrowed my options, energies, and desires. All the remaining members of my extremely small family are either physically or emotionally distant or dead. So much of what and so many of those on whom I used to rely for support and meaning are less robust or no longer here. I can no longer move furniture, heft a bag of cat litter, enjoy the quieting effect of Sarvangasana (shoulder stand pose), pick up a toddler and spin them around, or dance wildly, joyfully. I'm learning to be content with this narrower list of abilities and options.

In her manual, Hay advises that with any affliction, you ask yourself, "What could be the thoughts in me that created this?" Then, tell yourself, "I am willing to release the pattern in my consciousness that has created this condition." She offers a new thought pattern for each of the several hundreds of diseases and conditions she catalogues. Recite the one that addresses your affliction many times a day and then believe, really believe, that the healing process is already underway. For osteoporosis, she recommends the affirmation, "I can stand up for myself, and Life supports me in unexpected, loving ways." I don't doubt that true believers have been so nourished and strengthened by Hay's mantra that they've slowed, perhaps even halted, their progression from wherever they are to the fourth frame in the development of severe osteoporosis.

More than drugs, surgery, exercise, or affirmations, it's true belief that heals. A friend of mine faithfully takes a bisphosphonate for her osteoporosis. This woman, who teaches workshops on how to manifest one's desires and who, in fact, gave me my copy of Hay's New Age self-help manual, believes deep in her bones that this drug is strengthening her. Each new scan shows an improvement in her bone density. "I take the alendronate and just trust that it's making me stronger," she says. I don't tell her about the difference between "relative risk reduction" (RRR), a comparative statistic that refers to the percentage of the decrease in risk of fracture achieved by the group receiving the bisphosphonate over that of a group that hasn't, and "absolute risk reduction" (ARR), a straightforward statistic that quantifies the actual risk of something happening (in this case, a fracture) in the group receiving bisphosphonate with a number or absolute difference. I don't tell her that according to a review conducted by the American College of Physicians, the RRR of hip fractures in a group receiving bisphosphonate treatment for at least three years was 36%, while the ARR was only 0.6%. The latter number means that you must treat 167 patients for three years to prevent just one hip fracture. A 2022 Scottish study found that women who are informed only of the RRR of bisphosphonate treatment, a statistic which makes the treatment seem more effective than it actually is, are more willing to take it than women who are given the more realistic ARR. The statistic that my friend is working with is the RRR. But I suspect that the drug isn't helping her as much as her faith in it is. I won't interfere with anyone's faith that a healing is underway.

Repeating a potent seed thought can influence the course of one's disease and healing. But Hay's pleasant affirmations seemed rootless to me. If I'm to place my faith in a mantra, it must be grounded in something I trust. I found mine when I heard a sermon based on Isaiah 58. What the pastor focused on from that chapter is the type of fasting that God values—not a hypocritical or self-serving type but one that is genuine and righteous, a type of fasting that frees the oppressed, feeds the hungry, houses the unhoused, and more. But what seized and held me, as is always the case when God intends for me to take a scriptural promise or warning to heart, comes later in verse 11, which in the New King James Version reads, "The Lord will guide you continually, And satisfy your soul in drought, And strengthen your bones; You shall be like a watered garden, And like a spring of water, whose waters do not fail." When this verse captured my attention, I took it as a sign that the promise and the promiser will show me how, whether through weight resistance, drugs, affirmations, or some combination of those, to make the tree that I am strong enough to support ice-laden branches, to hold nests full of hawks or squirrels or flickers, to bend instead of break in the wind, and eventually, to become soil when my life has ended. Several times a day, I recite a word or phrase from this long verse, a fragment that recalls the whole, a mantra that is founded on something in which I have faith, a power beyond all powers. My next DEXA scan is months away, but I believe that my weak, dry, porous bones are becoming moister, sturdier, and solider. I believe, deep in my bones, that I *am* stronger.

<hr />

Most mornings I practice Vrksasana: it has become an essential part of my bone-building regimen. I press down through my foot so that I'm rooted, anchored, grounded and draw the earth's energy into my trunk and limbs, into my very bones. I reach into the heavens and bring the sky's energy into me. When I gaze at a spot on the wall, I'm immoveable. But because trees don't have fronts or backs, I expand my awareness, moving my eyes from side to side and imagining what's behind me. I sway and creak like a tree in the wind; and yet, I believe that I could stand like this until the sun is overhead. My eyes and throat are soft. I breathe gently, just as leaves do through their pores. I pull water. Gather light. Sprout leaves that rustle in the breeze. Lay down rings of sapwood that, at least for now, are moist and supple enough to bend; strong and solid enough not to break. In this well-watered garden that I've created, I settle into the strength, vitality, and stillness.

My Velleity

Most of the leaves on the pin oak in my front yard drop in the fall. But some don't. Those that cling to the branches withstand snow, wind, and ice. Come spring, swelling buds and emerging leaves push off the dry, brown ones. If leaves were people, I'd describe the new ones as eager and determined. But it's harder to identify the attitudes of the old ones that are slow to let go. Persistent? Stubborn? Hopeful? Hopeless? Lacking in imagination, initiative, or will?

〰〰〰

Recently I discovered a word that names a feeling I've become quite familiar with: "velleity," a wish or inclination that isn't strong enough to nudge or push me into action. "Velle," Latin for "to will, to wish, to be willing" is the weakest form of volition—an indolent, lazy, decaffeinated form of desire. Velleity, then, is an impulse or inclination that hasn't ripened into intent or action. An "incomplete willing," is how theologian Thomas Aquinas described it. The paralysis of velleity might be caused by self-doubt, laziness, ennui, angst, or fear of commitment, consequences, or regret.

I doubt that I'd have noticed this word had I encountered it a decade or two ago, when I more easily and willingly acted on at least some of my intentions. But when I was flipping through Simon Hertnon's *Endangered Words: A Collection of Rare Gems for Book Lovers* at the public library last November, the entry for velleity leapt off the page. "I cannot imagine there are too many other English words," Hertnon wrote, "that so accurately describe such a pervasive condition."

On November 29 I was certain that my dignified tabby's further decline, which had begun in August with a respiratory infection, was inevitable and that his suffering might already be more than he could bear. But nine days would pass before my willingness was complete enough for me to act.

The process by which those leaves on my pin oak overwinter on the branches is "marcescence," a word whose silky whispers are beautiful to the ear and the tongue. The term is derived from the Latin *marcescere*, which means "to wither, languish, droop, decay, pine away." Marcescent leaves wither but do not drop in the autumn.

I've been reading about how this process works. Decreasing light in the autumn triggers chemical changes within the abscission or separation zone at the base of the leaf stalk. This gives rise to two different layers of cells. One layer stops the flow of water and nutrients, causing the leaf to fall from the branch by its own weight. The other layer, comprised of a fatty, corky material, seals the wounds of separation. The resulting leaf scars are lovely to behold, since the severed vessels that carry food and water between the branch and the leaf stem appear as hearts, dots, crescents, or peculiar little faces. Some people can identify a tree based solely on these scar bundle patterns. But when the abscission layer doesn't form, the dry leaf remains on the tree where it shakes or trembles in the winter wind, as if it's forgotten what it was supposed to do or lost its motivation.

Though I lacked the will to haul the Christmas tree up from the basement and assemble it the day after Thanksgiving as I usually do, it was my craving for more light that eventually broke my inertia. On December 6, a morning when I wasn't mentally sharp enough to write coherent, much less insightful comments on my students' essays because of a too-wakeful night, I set up the tree. It was a scaled-back version of what I usually do: two instead of three strands of lights; just the shiny, reflective ornaments but none of the construction paper, string, and popsicle stick handicrafts that my son and daughter had made as children. During the past fifteen Advent seasons, the cat dozed beneath the metal branches, nestled among the presents. But this year, he slept on a rug in front of the living room heating vent, his breath whistling and rattling.

When I finally turned the page on my "Modern Women Artists from the Museum of Modern Art" calendar on December 7—a sad, gray day—it was to Helen Frankenthaler's 1993 woodcut "Radius." I so yearned to be embraced by her vortex of vibrant, swirling greens that I dove in, aimed straight for the tiny crimson pool and the handful of burning yellow-white stars at the other end of the tunnel.

Most of the deeply lobed, bristle-tipped leaves clinging to my pin oak are on the lower branches on the south side, where the wind, rain, and snow don't hit as hard. This is also true of other pin oaks in my neighborhood. But on one neighbor's tree, there appears to be full foliage on some of the lower branches—full, though dry and brown, as if something's gone terribly wrong with this tree.

The cat and I could have avoided a share of our suffering had I been able to act upon what I knew when I first knew it. In this case, my velleity is a hard sin to forgive. But perhaps it wasn't velleity but love and hope that led me to pry open his mouth and shoot food and medicine down his throat with a syringe many times a day, even as he grew thinner and weaker, even as he lost the will to pummel blankets, skitter a foil ball across the hardwood floor, or clean the dribbled food off his fur. Or perhaps it was ignorance, since I sincerely believed that I could make him better. For these well-intentioned motives, I forgive myself. So, too, if my velleity and whatever suffering it may have caused kept me from making an impulsive decision with irreversible consequences. But what strengthened my will enough that I could finally admit that it was time to end his life wasn't love or hope or an ethical conviction or a reasoned choice. It was exhaustion. My old friend and I were simply worn out.

After the vet and I ended the life of my sweet, smart, loyal companion on December 8, I had the good sense to strip and wash every fabric surface that he'd slept on and empty his hairs from the vacuum cleaner, since I'm prone to fetishizing that which was physically associated with a departed loved one—like the coral, snap-up robe that my mother changed out of on the morning the ambulance took her to the hospital. Four days later, she died in a hospice facility, while I slept in the recliner at her side. I still keep the robe in a plastic bag on a shelf in my closet. It's been many years since I've looked at it, and even longer since I buried my face in it. But I like knowing that it's there.

The rug that my cat slept on in front of the living room heating vent and where I force fed him food and medicine was a reminder that I didn't want of the sad final weeks of his life. As I drove home from the vet's office, I planned on rolling up the rug and stuffing it in the garbage can.

Because of its marcescence, my pin oak doesn't fit neatly into the category of evergreen or deciduous trees. "Everciduous," I've heard the trees in this classification gray area called, or the "not so deciduous deciduous trees." One source says that in an evolutionary sense, the marcescent oaks, beeches, and hornbeams are mid-journey between their fully evergreen past and their fully deciduous future. But another source says that deciduous trees aren't more evolved than the evergreens. Rather, the two types of trees are adapted to different environments.

Because evergreens don't drop all their leaves at once, they have an advantage over deciduous trees in that their needles remain photosynthetic longer. But the maples, apples, ashes, cottonwoods, and other deciduous trees have an advantage over evergreens because by dropping their leaves, they reduce the water loss and frost damage that they experience during the colder part of the year while increasing their photosynthetic efficiency during the warmer part.

By releasing some of their leaves in the spring when the growing tree most needs the decomposing organic material, marcescent trees increase their survival odds over those trees that drop all their leaves in the fall. And, too, because the dry, brown clinging leaves have fewer nutrients and are harder to digest than softer, moister green ones, browsing deer stay away from the tree, which means that the marcescent tree's new twigs and buds are more likely to become leaves and shoots in the spring. But deer don't roam my neighborhood, and Rich, my lawn care guy, collects and takes away the leaves wherever they fall.

~~~~~

It was on a Wednesday that I ended my cat's life and that I vowed to dispose of the rug. But there was no hurry since the garbage haulers come on Mondays. So instead of taking the rug to the trash, I draped it over a railing on the deck. I found it comforting to know that if I wanted to, I could wrap myself in the rug, food spatters, gray hairs, drool, and all. But by the time Monday arrived, I couldn't part with the rug where the cat had spent so many of his final days. Nine months later, the rug still hangs over the deck railing. While the ability to take bold, decisive action is essential and admirable, so, too, is the ability to know when one should hold back. Having a word for that type of discernment would make it easier for me to claim and contemplate such motives.

If I selected, say, fourteen to sixteen essays from the thirty or so that I've written (and, in many cases, published) in the past several years, found a theme to pull them together and figured out, as Leslie Jamison says in a *Longreads* interview, "what sort of journey I was gonna take the reader on in the course of the book," sequenced those essays, revised them accordingly, wrote a preface and a rather mysterious, rather revealing title, I could submit the manuscript for publication. Of course, I won't make money from it or be in demand as a speaker, since collections of essays rarely spark much attention. But I'll probably win or at least place in some book contests, and even better, my essays will find readers who will be touched by them. I might even hear from a few of those readers.

With each of my other books, the closer I came to completing them, the greater my inspiration and momentum. But my relationship with the creation of this book is profoundly different. It's not that I have writer's block, because I write almost every day, have written enough material to fill two books, and have ideas for several other book projects. It's not that I'm opposed to going public with my writing. In fact, I relish reader feedback—at least in most cases. And it's not that these essays, which both tangle and untangle, both complicate and clarify, are neither authoritative nor conclusive. Rather, my apathy concerns the time and effort involved in preparing my writing for publication, an enterprise that always takes far longer than I expect. And yet, it's an enterprise that I find pleasurable. So, why can't I discipline myself to complete this book? "The COVID Effect," one friend suggested. "Lots of people are wondering why bother with anything when a pandemic can change everything." "Aging," said another. "At this point in our careers, we aren't as driven by worldly success as we used to be." Both explanations contain truth. But I sense that something deeper is immobilizing me.

After considering what it would take to complete this manuscript, I select a book from the tall stack that I brought home from the public library and head for the couch, usually to be joined by the cat. I only feel a twinge of guilt over my lack of drive, my velleitousness, and that I'm pouring my attention into someone else's book instead of my own.

~~~~~

When I opened my office window, the cat used to leap onto the sill to watch the squirrels, birds, and fluttering leaves in the pin oak tree. In later years when his joints were stiffer, he'd climb into the rocking chair and from there, climb onto the windowsill. But during his last autumn, if I saw him eyeing the open window, I'd gently lift him and place him on the sill.

~~~~~

An old friend speaks often about his fear of isolation and meaninglessness. Whatever remedies I suggest aren't doable, aren't comfortable, aren't a satisfying replacement for what he's lost or expects to lose. Once, I encouraged him to make a list of ten things he'd do if he weren't afraid. I was astonished that he completed the exercise and even more by his insightfulness. Clearly, he knew what to do to create a more engaged, meaningful, and consequential life. Yet he hasn't acted on any of the items on his list, whether volunteering to translate documents for asylum seekers at the U.S.-Mexico border or accompanying his grandson on a Cub Scout campout or becoming more expressive of his emotions. Perhaps my halfhearted friend can't imagine a life that is larger and richer than the one he's enduring. Perhaps his desire for fullness isn't strong enough to nudge or push him into action.

I've grown weary of our conversations about inaction, anxiety, and regret, and yet I understand my friend's paralysis. Though I've dreamed about being an energy healer for at least twenty years, it's only now that I'm bringing the dream into being through study, certification, and the creating of a space for my practice. But will I be bold enough to take the biggest step of all—seeking clients? Though I dream of moving to a place with milder winters and more socially, politically, and environmentally enlightened people than Nebraska (there are many options!), I haven't taken the essential steps of picking the place, thinning out my possessions, and putting my house on the market. Though I can imagine shifting a pleasant, platonic friendship with a kind, smart, wholehearted, though decidedly quirky man who is adept at expressing his emotions into something physical and romantic, I haven't said the words or taken the actions that would make that happen. Like my half-hearted friend, I'm not yet ready to exchange what is bland though familiar and seemingly safe for the unknown but potentially zesty and rewarding.

The December 9th email from a student who thanked me for being so kind to them this semester and who assured me that they'll never forget my class was as gratifying and enlivening as turning the page to Helen Frankenthaler's green tunnel. I admire this student who changed their gender, name, and pronouns a few weeks into the semester with no apologies or justifications. That I should be so bold and confident about the changes I desire. And maybe I was at their age.

"Just do it": an antonym for velleity.

~~~~~

Because of the bird songs, the floral and damp earth fragrances, and the bright, new greens of early spring, I've never noticed the both/and moment when there are green buds and brown leaves on the same branch of my pin oak. Nor have I witnessed the final letting go of last year's leaves.

~~~~~

While I'm not yet able to complete my book of ravels, I was able to write an essay about the loss of my cat. I liken this to cleaning out my bedroom closet when it's my basement, which is stacked with boxes that I haven't looked in for years, that I should be attending to. And yet, it's pleasing and useful to have an orderly closet with fewer clothes.

Even though I'm weary of listicle essays, that was the form I grabbed when I set out to write about my cat's long decline and death, since I wasn't yet ready to write directly about that loss or to create a fitting form and design for my ideas. Then, all I could do was take a clump of experience, break it into parts and number those pieces. I couldn't yet recognize the many connections that I sensed were in the story and so, as the authors of listicle essays are wont to do, I left that up to my readers. But as I ruminated over my list, I cut some items and thickened others into paragraphs or entire sections. I reordered the fragments again and again so that they presented a storyline and thoughts that were more developed, cohesive, and reflective. With each reordering, I renumbered the items until finally, I deleted the numbers. In short, I tricked my velleitous self into writing a real essay. Could I trick myself into finishing my book? Could I trick myself or my half-hearted friend into living with more gusto?

~~~~~

Studies by neuroscientists, psychologists, and other investigators of human behavior show that by possessing a wide range of words to accurately and precisely name our emotions, we can better regulate them, which benefits our physical and mental health. "Affect labelling" it's called, and here's how it works: When we have a strong, negative emotional response to an experience, it tends to activate the "alarm system" situated deep in the amygdala. But when we put our feelings into words, an area in the prefrontal cortex intervenes, dampening the reaction of the amygdala and other limbic regions, thus lowering our stress (or distress) levels. "Emodiversity," the ability to experience and recognize a wide variety and relative abundance of discrete emotions, enables those who possess it to respond to their experiences with more awareness, perhaps even wisdom and skill, than those that lack this attribute. Studies show that emodiverse people experience less inflammation, fewer symptoms of depression and anxiety, and require fewer medical visits than those that lack this quality.

Almost everyone can recognize and label the six basic emotions—fear, anger, happiness, sadness, disgust, and surprise. But most of us need help with what neuroscientist Lisa Feldman Barrett calls "Emotional granularity," the ability to name our feelings with a high degree of specificity and precision. "Perhaps the easiest way to gain [such an ability] is to learn new words," she advises. "Words seed your concepts, concepts drive your predictions, predictions regulate your body budget . . . and your body budget determines how you feel." "Body budget" is Barrett's metaphor for "allostasis," the process by which the body responds to stressors in order to maintain or regain equilibrium—stressors like the loss of a loved one; a severe, prolonged stretch of cold, snow, and ice in dark January; change or the inability to change when life seems stagnant; the fear, disease, death, isolation, and upheaval of a worldwide pandemic.

In her blog entry, "In Search of Obscure Words for Even Rarer Feelings: The More Emotions We Can Name, The Better Off We'll Be," Tiffany Watt Smith, a cultural historian and author of *The Book of Human Emotions* and *Schadenfreude: The Joy of Another's Misfortune*, provides a list of names for emotions that aren't part of most people's repertoire but perhaps should be. Some of my favorites from Smith's list include: "umpty," a feeling of everything being "too much" and all in the wrong way, a term taken from a 1970s British cartoon; "awumbuk," a word from the Baining people of Papau New Guinea that names the emptiness you feel after your visitors leave; "amae," a Japanese word which roughly translates as "the pleasure of surrendering to another in perfect safety"; "ilinx," a term coined by the French sociologist Roger Caillois to name the elated disorientation or guilty pleasure you feel when you commit a minor, wanton act of destruction, such as kicking over the office recycling bin; and "toska," a Russian term which Vladimir Nabokov defines as "great spiritual anguish, often without a specific cause . . . a longing with nothing to long for, a sick pining, a vague restlessness."

By integrating such words into our vocabulary, we gain more than just the ability to precisely name what we're feeling. Naming the hollowness that follows the leave-taking of a guest you love invites you to consider what that person's presence brought to you and what their departure took from you. Identifying your state of mind as "velleity" invites you to consider what it is that you want and why you can't or won't act to give that to yourself. Turning marcescence into a metaphor and a human quality invites you to consider if withering but refusing to let go in the face of the harsh and inevitable circumstances is a moral failure, or if such endurance or tenacity is a commendable trait.

Acquiring more and finer names for our emotional states also increases our sensitivity and curiosity so that we become aware of emotional states that we don't yet have names for—like the feeling I sometimes get, even at my age, that I haven't yet fully and completely entered "real" life. If I had a name for this, how much easier it would be to recognize this delusion when it's holding sway over me. If I had a name for this, how much more likely I'd be to speak with others about their tactics for easing or jolting themselves out of denial and into a fuller embrace of the only life we have.

What's really at the root of my book-related velleity? While it's gratifying when the complementary copies of a new book with my name on the cover arrive at my front door, not one of my books have given me what I crave: more substantial, meaningful human connections than I now have; an integral place in a nourishing community. I have no reason to believe that an eighth book would provide either of those. In fact, writing a book is so solitary and consuming that it interferes with my ability to seek and find what I long for.

Various writers have addressed this aspect of the writing life. In Terri Gross's 1987 *Fresh Air* interview with Joan Didion, Gross asked the writer about the alarming psychiatric report that she included in the first essay in her 1979 collection, *The White Album*. The psychiatrist interpreted the Rorschach test that he'd given Didion as

> describing a personality in process of deterioration with abundant signs of failing defenses and increasing inability of the ego to mediate the world of reality and to cope with normal stress . . . Emotionally, patient has alienated herself almost entirely from the world of other human beings. Her fantasy life appears to have been virtually completely preempted by primitive, regressive libidinal preoccupations many of which are distorted and bizarre.

Didion was astonished by this report, since she was sure that she hadn't had a mental breakdown. Rather, she believed that the seemingly bizarre behaviors she was exhibiting were the result of her being engrossed in the writing of her 1970 novel, *Play It As It Lays*. Her answers to the psychiatrist's questions "came out of that mood rather than my own." Didion explained to Gross that when you're writing a novel, "you're alienated from the world of other people. You just have these imaginary playmates who you spend the day with. And once you're deeply into it, you kind of resent it when you have to go out and go out to dinner and talk to other people when you find them an intrusion into this imaginary world. It's a peculiar hazard of writing novels."

Didion's comment is perceptive. But I must qualify it. The withdrawal from the world of other people that can accompany one's total absorption in the workings of the imagination is also a "peculiar hazard" of an intense engagement in any genre of imaginative writing, whether memoir, collections of essays or poems, a play, or immersive literary journalism. I know this because I've experienced the bumpy transition when shifting my attention from utter absorption with one of my creations back into the ordinary world. On occasion, the reentry has been jarring or disorienting. But as much as I love my forays into the world of imagination and craft, I admit that now they don't captivate or satisfy me as much as engagement in what Didion's psychiatrist calls "the world of other human beings."

Velleity can be an adversary or foe. But it can also be an ally or savior if it keeps you from doing what you don't really want to do. My book-related velleity reveals to me my true desires Rather than finish my book, I want to write essays simply when it pleases me. Rather than finish my book, I want to more frequently join the lively couple across the street for beverages and conversation on their patio. Rather than finish my book, I want to join a book club, something I've never felt that I had time for. Rather than finish my book, I want to invite my half-hearted friend to join me in naming and expressing our emotions with each other. Rather than finish my book, I want to create a studio by giving away the furniture in the spare bedroom, painting the walls the palest lavender, buying a massage table and positioning it in the center of the room, and hanging a print of Helen Frankenthaler's "Radius" on the wall. Then I'll invite clients into my studio, invite them into my life and me into theirs.

<hr>

When I awakened in the wee hours of the night on December 11, my first thought was that the sweet, old cat wasn't dozing on his rug in front of the living room heating vent. Because of my decision and action, he was dead, his ashes sprinkled at the pet cemetery, wherever that is. I was so ferociously homesick for him that I got up and wandered around the house.

The memory of one death ushers in the memories of so many

others. In the past few years, I've lost two friends of about my age within months of each other, a longtime neighbor, and an elderly uncle and his wife. These were deaths that I understood. But when my father died sixteen years ago, I was perplexed. Since three states and parts of two others separated him and me, I only saw him two or three times a year; he'd never learned to email and was a terse phone conversationalist. While I grieved the loss of this man I'd always known, this man who'd changed my diapers, who'd changed my son's diapers, and whose bedside I sat by during his final days, I wondered exactly what I was missing after he died, since during the past several decades he'd been but a small and distant part of my daily life. (What word names the loss of a close yet faraway or disembodied presence?) Even though my mother wasn't part of my daily life in a physical sense, when she died it was clear what I'd be missing. In addition to our bi- or triannual visits and our email, text, and Facebook contact, she and I talked at length by telephone almost every day during the decade following my father's death. We were each other's confidantes. When I saw her in person, I'd study with wonder her thickly drawn eyebrows; her hair, thinner and faded with age, though still red; her mildly bow-legged walk; her arthritic fingers shelling peas or pushing food onto her fork with a chunk of bread; her tendency to while away the afternoon while snuggled into her recliner with her cat and dog and a good novel; her delight as she and her puckish boyfriend kidded each other (glib, jokey insults and sexual innuendo). Because of our decades together, I found all of this as familiar as my own skin. And yet, because of the distance created by miles and years, I also found it rather strange.

Unlike my parents, my esteemed feline companion was always physically there, always awaiting my return, intensely watching me with his green eyes. I couldn't read, write, grade essays, or watch television without him pressed against my side. Every morning, I scooped and carried his feces and urine to the garbage. When I did my reclining yoga postures, he'd bump my forehead with his or roll onto his back or side and squirm until I petted him. When I showered, he waited for me on the bath rug. He was there for every holiday, every birthday, every sorrow, every joy. We rarely discussed politics or religion. Our tastes in music were nearly identical. He liked some of my friends and kin but snubbed others. Now, almost anywhere I go in my house, I glimpse him there.

I ended my 3 a.m. wander at a window in my home office where my office mate used to bask in the sun. During the last few weeks of his life, he'd drag himself from his rug in front of the living room heating vent and up the half flight of stairs—unless I heard his thumps and got there in time to carry him—so he could doze in the sun. During the last days of his life, I knew how far gone he was because instead of following the warm bars of sunlight inching across the carpet, he remained where I'd placed him, even though it had grown colder and darker there. Now that he's gone, I'm left with a bundle of emotions, some that I can name (grief, relief, regret, and gratitude) and some that I can only describe (my willingness to remember the broad sweep but none of the fine details of his dying or those of my parents; the weave of guilt and delight I feel when I consider how completely the black kitten that I adopted from the no-kill shelter on December 19 has filled the void left by the dear, old one's departure).

Earlier in the evening of my 3 a.m. ramble, I'd seen a quarter moon caught in the branches of the pin oak like an unanswered question, a big, fat regret, an unclaimed reward. But at this time of night and from this vantage point, the moon was where I could no longer see it. What the tree was embracing in its branches were sparse, dry, brown curled leaves; two squirrel nests, messy clots built from pin oak leaves and twigs, each on a high, outer limb; and burning stars.

ACKNOWLEDGMENTS

I gratefully acknowledge the care and attention that the editors of the following publications gave my essays:

"The Renoir." *Still Point Arts Quarterly* (2013)

"Still Life with Peaches." *Georgia Review* (2014) Notable Essay Citation, *Best American Essays of 2014*

"Daily Bread." *Rock & Sling: A Journal of Witness* (2016)

"Namestaker." *Blood Orange Review* (2017)

"Leaving the Body." First Prize, 2018 "Leaving" writing contest, *Hospital Drive.*

"Free Samples." *The Boiler* (2018)

"In the Place of Their Exile." *Ascent* (2019)

"Common Magic." *The Midnight Oil* (2021)

"Fleet." *Windhover* (2023)

"My Velleity." *West Branch* (2023)

"Doves for Dinner." In *Good Eats: 32 Writers on Eating Ethically* (2024)

Sky Songs: Meditations on Loving a Broken World
by Jennifer Sinor

In the Shadow of Memory
by Floyd Skloot

Secret Frequencies: A New York Education
by John Skoyles

The Days Are Gods
by Liz Stephens

Phantom Limb
by Janet Sternburg

This Jade World
by Ira Sukrungruang

The Sound of Undoing: A Memoir in Essays
by Paige Towers

When We Were Ghouls: A Memoir of Ghost Stories
by Amy E. Wallen

Knocked Down: A High-Risk Memoir
by Aileen Weintraub

Yellowstone Autumn: A Season of Discovery in a Wondrous Land
by W. D. Wetherell

This Fish Is Fowl: Essays of Being
by Xu Xi

To order or obtain more information on these or other University of Nebraska Press titles, visit nebraskapress.unl.edu.